"A perceptive and fascinating study of the work of one of America's finest young adult novelists."
—Norma Klein
Author of *Mom, the Wolfman and Me*

"The talent and craft of one of the major writers for young adults are explored in this significant addition to a series that stands alone in its contribution to the field of young adult literature."
—Christy Tyson
Young Adult Coordinator,
Spokane Public Library

SALLY HOLMES HOLTZE is a free-lance editor and critic of literature written for children and young adults. A former reviewer and book review editor for the *Horn Book Magazine* and *School Library Journal,* she is currently series editor for *Junior Authors and Illustrators.* Ms. Holtze lives in New York City.

PRESENTING

Norma Fox Mazer

Sally Holmes Holtze

Published by
Dell Publishing
a division of
Bantam Doubleday Dell Publishing Group, Inc.
666 Fifth Avenue
New York, New York 10103

Photographs and captions kindly provided by Norma Fox Mazer.

ISBN: 0-440-20486-0

RL: 9.4

Reprinted by arrangement with Twayne Publishers

Printed in the United States of America

December 1989

10 9 8 7 6 5 4 3 2 1

OPM

To the memory of my father,
Max Edward Holmes
1924–1985

Contents

Preface

Writing a critical study of a popular young adult author immediately presents two questions. The first is: Does the subject merit an entire book of critical examination? In this case she is an author selling thousands of mass-market paperbacks a year, with wide popular appeal, as opposed to a writer of more "literary" or complex novels, books that win literary awards and sell a few thousand copies before going out of print. The second question is: How can one study an evolving artist whose technique varies with every book and who improves with every book? Wouldn't such a study be obsolete with the publication of her next novel?

The consideration of these questions has led me to decide, with much enthusiasm, that a close look at the work of a novelist like Norma Fox Mazer is the very least we should offer to librarians, educators, students, and other readers of literature for young adults. At American Library Association meetings and in seminars, panels, and workshops across the country, as well as in articles in journals and chapters in books, individuals who work with literature for young adults lambaste and lecture upon the lack of serious critical attention directed toward books for children and young adults. The opportunity to apply standards of literary criticism to all of Mazer's writing results in rich revelations, not only in traditionally scrutinized areas of style, theme, characterization, plot, and setting, but also in the areas unique to the study of a current young adult author, such as the vital appeal of Mazer to her readers, and the ground-breaking aspects of some of her work in a body of literature that is still quite young.

Concerning the second question, while Norma Fox Mazer is an innovator, an experimenter in her books, her independent, strong young female protagonists and her themes of finding one's own way and working through problems rather than succumbing to defeat pervade her work. The harmony of her concerns and the strong encouraging examples she portrays to her readers bind her books together like the songs on a thematic record album; like singles, they can be experienced and enjoyed on their own, but a far richer experience awaits readers who find most or all of Mazer's books. Consider the stylistically immature yet powerful and moving *A Figure of Speech;* the superb collections of short stories; the cinematically written, timely, and suspenseful *Taking Terri Mueller;* and the sophisticated techniques in the use of dialogue and point of view used in her recent novel *Three Sisters.* As diverse as her topics seem to be, and as varied as her ways of telling a story are, we find recurring themes and elements: psychologically strong girls and young women; working-class settings in which the family is usually important to the whole picture; and the courageous confrontation of problems, dilemmas, and choices.

Though one hopes that Mazer will write more books, it is not frivolous to draw the line at one point and to examine the body of her work, for it informs us not only about the state of her development and achievement, but about the state of current young adult literature.

An examination of Mazer's work prompts a look back at the history of the genre of realistic fiction written specifically for young adults, a genre that has its roots in the work of novelists of the 1940s and 1950s, such as Florence Crannell Means and Mary Stolz, and has as its direct ancestors the first novels of Paul Zindel, S. E. Hinton, and John Donovan. Some of the first realistic novels written for young adults were commissioned by editors of juvenile books, an example being *The Pigman* by Paul Zindel, who had written a Pulitzer Prize–winning play about a young woman protagonist, *The Effect of Gamma Rays on Man-in-the-Moon Marigolds,* and was asked to try writing a novel for young adults. When Mazer's first novel, *I, Trissy,* was published in 1971, and when *A Figure of Speech* came out in 1973, the ground for realism in young adult fiction had been broken. S. E. Hinton's *The Outsiders* had been published in 1967, along with Ann Head's

Mr. and Mrs. Bo Jo Jones; The Pigman came out in the following year, and novels by John Donovan came out in 1967 and 1971. Mazer's first two novels fit squarely into the emerging genre. *I, Trissy* was precocious in that its subject was a strong, independent, and funny character coming to terms with the realization that her parents were truly separated. *A Figure of Speech* features Jenny Pennoyer, whose parents try to place her beloved grandfather in a nursing home against Jenny's strong objections. The middle-class setting, the sometimes harsh facts of life, and the lack of a happy ending are earmarks of the steadily increasing numbers of books of realistic fiction for young adults.

It is an exciting and rewarding task to evaluate the importance of Mazer's fiction in the current literature for young adults. Her development as a novelist is parallel not only to the development of concurrently published genre fiction, but to the rising awareness of feminism in the 1970s and the repercussions of that awareness upon society in general and on teenagers in particular.

A study of Mazer's works shows that she continues the genre of realistic fiction written for young adults and that she influences readers and other writers; and one begins to understand her unique place in young adult fiction. By an examination of her strong, lively, and independent protagonists; her varied prose styles and techniques; her goals in writing; her appealing settings of middle-class family life; and the conflicts and problems her characters face, I hope to add to that understanding of her unique position.

• • •

I am very grateful to Norma Fox Mazer for her generosity in granting several interviews. Not only was she generous with her time but with the wealth of material she provided about herself, her family, and her books. Unattributed remarks and quotations from Norma Fox Mazer derive from her interviews and correspondence with me.

I would like to thank my editor, Athenaide Dallett, for her great contributions to this book, which include expert guidance in its organization, wisdom and originality in solving problems, and kindness, patience, and encouragement for her author.

I would like to thank Ron Brown, general editor of Twayne's Young Adult Authors Series, for choosing Norma Fox Mazer as a subject for the series and for having the confidence in me to ask me to write it.

I would also like to thank Karen Gray for her support and encouragement and Heather Cameron for her kindness.

Chronology

1931 Born Diane Norma Fox 15 May in New York City.

1935 Father blacklisted after a strike, family moves to Glens Falls, where maternal grandmother has a bakery.

1946 At 15, meets Harry Mazer, aged 21.

1948 Meets Harry Mazer again.

1949 Attends Antioch College.

1950 Marries Harry Mazer. Accepted at Hunter College. Moves to New York City, leaves after six months for Schenectady, New York.

1953 Daughter Anne born.

1955 Son Joseph born.

1957 Moves to Syracuse. Begins three years of night school, University College of Syracuse University.

1958 Daughter Susan born.

1963 Daughter Gina born. Becomes a full-time free-lance writer, writing pulp fiction for magazines.

1971 *I, Trissy.*

1973 *A Figure of Speech.*

1974 *A Figure of Speech* nominated for a National Book Award.

1975 *Saturday, the Twelfth of October* published, and wins a Lewis Carroll Shelf Award.

1976 January *Top of the News,* "Comics, Cokes, & Censorship."

Dear Bill, Remember Me? and Other Stories published, and is named an Outstanding Book of the Year 1976 by the *New York Times,* a Best Book for Young Adults by the American Library Association (ALA), and a Notable Book by the ALA, and receives the Christopher Award.

1977   *The Solid Gold Kid,* with co-author Harry Mazer.

1978   *The Solid Gold Kid* named a Children's *Choice* Book and a Best Book for Young Adults by the ALA.

1979   *Up in Seth's Room* published, and is named a Best Book for Young Adults by the ALA.

1980   *Mrs. Fish, Ape, and Me, the Dump Queen.*

1981   *Taking Terri Mueller* (paperback original) published, and wins the 1981 Edgar Allan Poe Award for best juvenile mystery.

1982   *When We First Met* published, and made into a film presented by the Learning Corporation of America and shown on the HBO cable channel. *Summer Girls, Love Boys.*

1983   *Someone to Love.*

1984   *Someone to Love* named a Best Book for Young Adults by the ALA. "I, Hungry Hannah Cassandra Glen . . ." published in *Sixteen: Short Stories by Outstanding Young Adult Writers.*

1984   *Downtown. Supergirl,* novel based on the screenplay.

1985   *Downtown* named an Outstanding Book of the Year by the *New York Times* and a Best Book for Young Adults by the ALA.

1986   *Three Sisters. A, My Name Is Ami.* "Tuesday of the Other June" published in *Short Takes: A Short Story Collection for Young Readers.* Receives California Young Readers Medal for *Taking Terri Mueller* and the Iowa Teen Award for *When We First Met.*

1987   *After the Rain. B, My Name Is Bunny.*

1. Norma Fox Mazer
and the Roots of Realism

Trissy Beers, the heroine of Norma Fox Mazer's first novel, *I, Trissy,* and the daughter of separated parents, finds a note that she's not supposed to see. It is left with a homemade chocolate cake in her father's bachelor apartment. The note is from a woman, obviously one who is used to the apartment, and evidently one who has spent the night with Trissy's father.

What does Trissy do? She does the kind of thing heroines of books for children and young adults didn't generally do in the year *I, Trissy* was published; she plunges both hands into the cake, squeezes and mashes it, and then smears chocolate frosting handprints all over the walls of the apartment.

Few heroines before Trissy strayed as far as she does from more conventional heroines: less passionate protagonists who never came up against the kind of emotionally upsetting situation that Trissy did and who would not have reacted that way if they had. Some children's authors before Mazer had written on realistic topics and given their protagonists first-person narratives to describe their problematical lives. But when *I, Trissy* and Norma Fox Mazer's other early works appeared, it was still unusual to find strong, independent protagonists describing their very contemporary problems.

I, Trissy is a book for a younger audience than most of Mazer's novels, which fall into the young adult category, usually defined as books for readers twelve and older. However, the book shares with Mazer's later works the realism that was prevalent among young adult novels emerging at the time of its publication, as well as strong, independent heroines and the innovative style of her young adult novels. To see how Mazer is an innovative contributor to the genre of young adult literature, it is helpful to examine some of the history of the genre as well as what books were available when her first books appeared.

During the 1930s and the 1940s some books were published that showed teenage protagonists in contemporary, realistic settings, facing unusual problems. The novels of Florence Crannell Means are extraordinary forerunners in the young adult genre. In Means's *Shuttered Windows,* published in 1939, the protagonist is a black junior in high school who confronts poverty in South Carolina, where she moves to live near her great-grandmother; her perspective on the black South is revealed to readers. Both the subject matter and the close identification with the reader made the book different from lighter fare for teenagers. Means leaves some aspects of racial strife out of the book, which is occasionally trite and sentimental, but the extraordinary author was ahead of her time and a trailblazer in fiction for young adults.

Maureen Daly's popular *Seventeenth Summer,* which came out in 1942, is often considered the first "junior novel" of quality. The book, according to one critic, "Shows adolescent life, not from the adults' viewpoint as they look back, but rather from the adolescents' viewpoint. . . . Her book succeeds because it parallels the emotions of many teenage girls."[1] *Seventeenth Summer* represented a new approach to the junior novel, for teenagers' problems are "taken as seriously as they are by the young people experiencing them." Furthermore, the book "gave a truthful picture of adolescent life: beer parties and blanket parties; the girl who makes the mistake of dating a boy with a bad reputation. . . ."[2]

Other writers such as Mary Stolz explored teenagers' problems, such as one girl's concern with being overweight; her *In a Mirror* was published in 1953. But a real landmark in young adult literature was published about that time; in 1951 J. D. Salinger's *Catcher in the Rye,* the realistic story of an adolescent who runs away from his prep school just before the beginning of Christmas vacation, has become a young adult classic, yet it was written for adults. Realistic fiction written specifically for young adults did not mature for another sixteen years.

Kenneth L. Donelson and Alleen Pace Nilsen, in their *Literature for Today's Young Adults,* call the year 1967 the birth of the new realism[3] in fiction for teenagers; in that year S. E. Hinton's *The Outsiders,* published expressly for young adults, appeared, along with Ann Head's *Mr. and Mrs. Bo Jo Jones,* which was published for adults but found its audience among young adults. *The Outsiders* concerns a fourteen-year-old boy who becomes involved in street-gang fighting. Ann Head's book concerns a pregnant girl who marries the child's father.

The numbers of realistic young adult novels quickly increased. They were characterized for the most part by controversial topics, middle-class settings, sometimes harsh realities of life, unhappy endings, and the points of view of the young protagonists, particularly in first-person narrative.

Some of the most popular, enduring giants of young adult literature were published in the five years after *The Outsiders* was. Paul Zindel's masterpiece, *The Pigman,* appeared in 1968; his *My Darling, My Hamburger* followed in 1969, along with John Donovan's *I'll Get There. It Better Be Worth the Trip.* Judy Blume's influential *Are You There, God? It's Me, Margaret.* was published in 1970, the year before *I, Trissy* was, and Norma Klein's *Mom, the Wolfman and Me* followed in 1972. The latter was similar to *I, Trissy* in that a girl confronts the problem of a parent's romance after the mother and father have split up.

One other book, a precursor of *I, Trissy,* bears mention in a discussion of Mazer's place in young adult literature. Though a book for younger readers, like *I, Trissy, Harriet the Spy* by Louise Fitzhugh shares characteristics of young adult realism. Published in 1964, it treats divorce, as *Trissy* treats separation. Harriet is defiant and strong, as is Trissy, though Trissy is a far more likable character; and Trissy's different conventions of writing—diary entries, newspaper articles—recall Harriet's notebook. The popular reception that *Harriet the Spy* received is proof that strong, independent protagonists were welcome additions to the available literature for children as well as for young adults.

How did Norma Fox Mazer come to write the kinds of books for young people that she did, at a time when the genre was just beginning? The story of her background and her life helps to explain how she came to write books that mean a great deal to her many readers.

Mazer's grandparents were all immigrants from Europe. Her father's parents, named Fox, came from the Ukraine, spent about eight years in England, and settled in New York City. Her grandfather's father, named Gorelic, had a bakery in the Polish village of Bialystock. His son, Mazer's maternal grandfather, emigrated to the United States, where he opened a bakery in Glens Falls, New York. Her grandfather "read books while the bread burned"; he had never wanted to be a baker. He spoke four or five languages, and probably would have liked to pursue an intellectual life, not concerning himself with the things of the world, but being a baker was the only way he could support his family. His wife was a practical person, able to run the business.

Mazer's legacy—"the whole weight of the past"—was of immigrant relatives who struggled and who were poor. Both of her parents had to leave school in the eighth grade to begin working. Her father, Michael Fox, was born in England in 1898. He married Jean Garlen, who was born in 1904. Both were great readers. Michael Fox was a quiet, introspective person. Jean Garlen Fox is an energetic woman with enormous vitality; at the age of eighty-two, she currently works as assistant coordinator for the Le Moyne College summer Elderhostel. The family left New York City in 1935 when Michael Fox was blacklisted for having participated in a strike. They went to Glens Falls, where Mrs. Fox's brother ran the family bakery, and Michael earned his living driving first a bread truck, then a milk truck. He was a "route man" whom customers liked. Mrs. Fox worked as a waitress and as a sales clerk. Economically, they were working-class people, but the family was traditionally highly literate. The couple had three daughters: Adele, born in 1926, followed by middle-child Norma in 1931, and Linda in 1937.

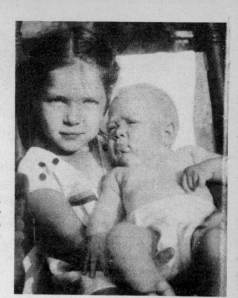

1937: Glens Falls, N.Y. Me with my baby sister, Linda, who was said to have such a ferocious scowl as an infant she scared the adults.

1937: Glens Falls, N.Y. My beautiful older sister, Adele, and me, reading as usual.

c. 1938: This is at a summer camp where my mother or possibly both my parents were working. I don't know who dressed me up; there was a summer theatre there and obviously the costume came from their wardrobe. Just as obviously, I doubt they let kids muck about in it without supervision.

c. 1939: Here I seem to be writing, while Adele is looking graceful and lovely.

1940: Bronx Park zoo. That's Linda, now about 3 years old, on the right.

c. 1941: One of my favorite pictures for some reason; maybe I think it's my character Trissy showing up in me at an early age. I'm in front; the other girl was someone I'd just met. It seems as if we were kindred spirits.

c. 1943: This is a photo that captures a very strong mental image I have of myself (as a watcher; in this case, watching the grownups) through a lot of my adolescence.

1970: Big jump in years: by this time my youngest is 7 years old and I'm at work on my first book, *I, Trissy*. My typewriter is right there at my elbow. At that time, with a houseful of kids, my "office" was in a corner of the bedroom.

1973: About the time *A Figure of Speech* was published and another favorite photo of mine; I feel as if it's related to the adolescent one of me.

Norma Fox Mazer, 1985.
Photograph by Mima Cataldo.

Norma Fox Mazer was born in New York City at a time when women stayed in the hospital for ten days after they gave birth. During this recuperation period for Mazer's mother, one of her nurses came into her room; her own name was Norma, and she said (mistakenly), "Mrs. Fox, I'm so thrilled you named your baby after me." Mazer characterizes her mother as not terribly assertive at this point, so the baby, who had been named Diane Norma Fox on her birth certificate, was called Norma.

Mazer remembers the working-class nature of her childhood; at the age of seven or eight, she met a girl whose family owned their own house. It had a fireplace, a screened-in porch; these things impressed Mazer. Her family lived in apartments; to her, the girl was rich.

Mazer grew up with books in the home; she taught herself to read before she went to school. As a child, she read books as varied as the Andrew Lang fairy-tale books *(The Blue Fairy Book, The Green Fairy Book)*, Nancy Drew mysteries, *Gulliver's Travels,* the Lambs' *Tales from Shakespeare,* and the books her parents were reading; there were no "young adult" books in those days. Of this indiscriminate reading, Mazer says, "I didn't get any factual education out of it. I don't know what I got out of it, except a lot of pleasure."

When Mazer was in third grade, she made up triplet brothers. To explain their absence, she told friends they were in the navy. Later, she decided to take up the use of her real first name and wrote "Diane" across the tops of her school papers. However, when the teacher called out "Diane," she just sat there, not answering, waiting for some real Diane to reply. Mazer considers this her first attempt at another personality.

Her imagination went unnoticed and unremarked upon by her teachers, as did her penchant to be "always scribbling"—descriptions, thoughts, diary entries, the beginning of stories. She remembers helping a friend with her composition, wondering why it was so hard for her. She was an excellent student in high school, but nobody ever said anything to her about her talent. Mazer herself makes a point of encouraging interested children to write. The only instance she remembers of another person recognizing her "writer's personality" was when a girlfriend exclaimed, "Norma Fox! What an imagination!"

Mazer was a special child, beginning to write creatively and receiving excellent grades in school, but not receiving any special attention from the school system and feeling that her intelligence was an unspoken, but definite, social hindrance. She was growing up in the 1930s and 1940s in a small town; the time and place were not conducive to a bright girl who sought to fit in, not stand out. Mazer was trying to be like everybody else, "to have all the right opinions, to be nice and to say all the nice things." She felt like an outsider—she says that being Jewish had something to do with it, but that since she felt that way even in the Jewish community, on reflection she thinks it also had a great deal to do with being bright and female. "There were lots of bright girls around, but it just wasn't the thing to be."

She also relates feeling alienated, to some extent, by her background.

> I think my parents never felt completely at home in this coun-
> try, because of their immigrant backgrounds, and I suppose I
> picked up on that. I don't know if I write about outsiders con-
> sistently, but I do an awful lot of it. Sometimes I'm conscious
> of it, and sometimes it's there when I'm not conscious of it. The
> whole working-class thing is also a very strong influence.

But there was something else, perhaps more important than being Jewish, or female, or bright, or even working-class, that set Mazer apart. It was her writer's temperament.

Being an observer by nature, Mazer was often misunderstood; though really shy and inhibited, she was seen differently by others. "People in my family thought I was aloof, cold, uninterested," she says. "I was watching everything that was going on around me. I think of myself that way: *watching, watching.*" As an outsider, she had to rely on herself, and she recalls the strength she felt at a young age: "I think that from the time I was very young I was the kind of person who had strength inside, but I was also very frightened; it took a long time to get past that layer of fear and to be independent and strong."

At the age of fifteen Norma Fox met her future husband, Harry Mazer. Her father was a friend of Harry Mazer's uncle, Max Mazer; the two men used to talk politics and go fishing together. However, although Harry visited his uncle in Glens Falls, Norma never met him there. She didn't meet him until he went to Union College in Schenectady after serving in World War II. He was twenty-one years old and Norma Fox was fifteen. She met Harry on a visit to her older sister. Harry drove Norma home after her visit, a distance of about thirty-five miles. She recalls telling her girlfriend, "I met this really handsome neat guy," but she did not see him again until two years later. In the fall of 1948 he and her older sister were both involved in the Progressive Party's presidential campaign for Henry Wallace, who had been Franklin D. Roosevelt's Secretary of Agriculture. Harry Mazer had graduated from Union College. Norma Fox was seventeen, and, she says, "he thought I was too young for him."

Norma went away to Antioch College in Yellow Springs, Ohio, but shocked her parents by leaving after only one semester to marry Harry. She was eighteen. She and Harry moved to New York City, where she was accepted at Hunter College. She found the noisy, crowded city difficult, so the couple moved upstate to Schenectady, where they started a family. Her first daughter, Anne (who is now a writer), was born in 1953; her son Joe (who has an engineering degree, but is presently a carpenter) followed in 1955; then came Susan (now an artist) in 1958; and finally Gina (a poet and writer who is now in college) was born in 1963, ten years to the day after Mazer's oldest daughter.

As her children grew, Mazer dreamed of being a writer. She kept notes on her first daughter's babyhood, and began to write short stories when her son was born. In 1957 the family moved to Syracuse, and she "knuckled down to writing an-hour-a-day-no-matter-what" in about 1960.

At the same time Harry Mazer, who had been working at a series of jobs—longshoreman, railroad worker, welder, iron worker, English teacher—also became serious about writing. For one year they got up at three in the morning and worked back-to-back at their desks, Norma at a portable manual typewriter. At seven when they heard the children stirring, she went out to make breakfast and Harry went off to the factory where he worked as a welder.[4]

Mazer wrote fiction for magazines like *Ingenue* and *Calling All Girls*, but received her first check as a writer for $1.50 for an animal quiz. As a "pulp fiction" writer, she wrote stories for women's romance magazines. She calls this her apprenticeship as a writer, a time during which she wrote and published close to half a million words every year. The years of intense writing developed her ability; she says she doesn't suffer from writer's block and goes eagerly to her desk every day, seven days a week. However, while the Mazers were able to support their family with their writing, the pay was not great: They used to joke that a garbage man in Syracuse made more money than both of them together.

After seven years of writing pulp, Mazer wrote her first book for children, *I, Trissy*. She sent it to her agent, who gave it to an editor at Delacorte, who bought it immediately. Mazer wanted to keep writing books, but had to continue writing pulp fiction to support the family; she and Harry Mazer would "trade months" so they could each spend some time on the kind of writing they really wanted to do.

I, Trissy comprises three weeks in the life of Trissy Beers, who bangs out the story of her parents' separation on a typewriter in first-person narrative, as well as in dramatic scenes, lists, compositions written for school, and mock newspaper articles. Mazer recalls that when she wrote the book she thought, "I'm using all these literary forms and people are going to really think this is great," but "of course nobody ever noticed."

Mazer calls her second novel, *A Figure of Speech*, the first real novel she wrote. Before she ever began chapter 1, she wrote two hundred pages of notes on the story, enough alone to make up a book. Its setting is a middle-class home in which the young protagonist, Jenny, battles against her family's efforts to place her grandfather in a nursing home. "All the time I was writing it, I was thinking, is this the way you write a novel? Is this what you do?" She recalls a crisis during the writing of the book, when she couldn't see her way out of a particular problem. She got so upset that she went to bed. She was "in a panic," but by the time she got up, she understood what she needed to do to make the novel work. She explains the feeling of "fear and terror" that came over her whenever she wrote. "I was just in a general state of fear for many years." Then she wrote her first collection of short stories (Mazer has two collections). "Somehow the whole process of writing many stories in a short period of time said to me, *You really are a writer.*" That was the first time she wholly accepted herself as a writer, and this was five years after *I, Trissy.*

It took her even longer to realize that not only was she a writer, but that she would never have to be or do anything else for her living. She had often comforted herself with the thought that if she couldn't succeed at writing she could always go out and get a job as a typist or a cashier. "The longer I wrote, the less appealing and less likely those choices seemed."

Mazer likes reading and writing contemporary fiction because, she says, realistic contemporary fiction deals with how other people live. "You've got your face right in somebody's window" is how she describes it. "You safely get to be a voyeur." She thinks a great deal about how other people live and cope. "I really think the world we live in is very horrible in a lot of ways," she says. "The pollution—the nuclear threat—all these things hit kids very hard." She thinks people need strength to deal with what goes on, and that it's "especially hard for kids today to grow up with a feeling of hope."

Life isn't easy, is the message that readers get from Mazer's books as they see her protagonists battle with large, very real problems in their lives, from Terri Mueller, who discovers that her father kidnapped her from her mother when she was a small child, to Cary Longstreet, who had vainly hoped that for her birthday she would be adopted by the last in a long succession of foster parents. Norma Fox Mazer is aware of the problems young people face. Yet this awareness does not overwhelm her so that she cannot enjoy the life she and her husband have made for themselves; to dig in the garden or to eat a piece of Harry's home-made bread are simple things from which she draws pleasure.

Some of Mazer's topics seem to come right from the pages of

newspapers; *When We First Met,* for instance, treats the topic of
drunken driving. However, according to Mazer, the theory that
her book could derive from only a newspaper article is incorrect
because "a book is much more complex than that." The closest
she has come to writing a book about a media-inspired topic, she
says, is *Up in Seth's Room,* in which she explored the topic of a
girl who chose *not* to have sexual intercourse with her boyfriend.
She had read that fifty-two percent of a certain segment of teenage
girls were sexually active. What about the other forty-eight percent, Mazer wondered. "That's a lot of kids."

She believes that, over the years, one can develop techniques
that help the writing, but that most of the process is mysterious,
and she says that the more at ease she is with herself as a writer,
the more mysterious it becomes. On the influence of reviews,
Mazer comments that she wishes she didn't read them. She says
that she wants to read really good things about her books, and
yet doesn't quite believe them, while negative reviews only con-
firm her worst opinion of herself. She still recalls a book review
of *Saturday, the Twelfth of October,* her third book, that bothered
her, particularly when Barbara Wersba, the reviewer, wonders
"why menstruation looms so largely in the plot," and why "biological realism is forced upon stories that do not need it."[5]

Mazer says she tries to keep a perspective on her work. She
feels that it is work, but it is also play. She looks at herself as
privileged to be able to make up stories for a living. When she
gets too concerned or too scared about herself as a writer, she
says to herself, come on, don't take yourself so seriously. The world
can spin without her artistic contribution, she feels, as it can
without the contributions of singers, artists, and other writers,
but, she says, "Would most of us want to spin without them?"

This particular writer lives in central New York State, in a
wonderful house made of cedar that is so near a creek that its
deck overhangs the water. When you sit on the deck, and look
up, the sky is almost obscured by the various greens of the trees'
leaves; the light plays on the leaves and you can see the greens
change as time passes. The forest all around the house hides tiny
wildflowers, only a few left in July when I visited. There's a

hammock on the desk, and Teddy the cat occasionally streaks by, hunting small game. The drive through the countryside to Mazer's house features vistas of rolling fields, black-and-white cows, trees, and sky; it recalls a passage from *Three Sisters,* when Karen "looked off at the land and the sky, thinking that there were some things you couldn't photograph, some things you couldn't even speak about."

There, the two writers live. Sometimes they travel, and Mazer likes to meet people when she does travel, but she doesn't do it often; Mazer loves her work, her house, and her garden, and misses them when she's away.

Norma Fox Mazer is a morning person; sometimes, having trouble sleeping, she gets up as early as 3:30, and as long as she's up, she gets started at her desk. Her desk is now part-computer. She has graduated from her old manual, even from electric typewriters, and no longer works with a ruler and stapler to revise as she used to. "I used to cut and staple, cut and staple. I'd have an arrow for a sentence or a paragraph to be moved and then a note to myself, 'put on page 12,' and on page 12 there'd be another note, 'move this paragraph to page 21.' Then the pages would get to be six layers deep before I was through." Now, she says, if nothing else, her computer saves her two weeks of hard typing to get her final manuscript ready for her editor.

In her leisure time Mazer likes to read. She likes contemporary fiction, such as Rosellen Brown's *Civil Wars,* Alison Lurie's *Foreign Affairs,* Sue Miller's *The Good Mother,* and Scott Spencer's *Walking the Dead,* all of which are favorites. She enjoys autobiographies—especially where the writer concentrates on his or her childhood. She also likes to read books about other cultures, such as Colin M. Turnbull's *The Forest People,* about the Pygmies of the Congo. Some young adult writers she especially enjoys are Rosa Guy, Marilyn Sachs, John Donovan, Norma Klein, Robert Cormier, and Harry Mazer.

In addition to reading, Mazer enjoys gardening tremendously, as one can see by walking up to her house. The garden is filled with countless varieties of strange and colorful plants, each one placed just so. The effect is not tidy, it's lush and wild, yet clearly the Mazers have taken a lot of care, for years, to choose what will thrive in each particular spot. A path near the house goes up to a field where there are even more plants—herbs and mundane plants and exotic varieties. The Mazers pick mushrooms, too, and Norma enjoys birdwatching.

Some of the lasting impressions one has of the physical presence of this very popular writer seem contradictory at first—but they aren't. She is at ease, laughing gently, but under her relaxation is an alertness for a bit of conversation that may intrigue her, a bit she grasps with eagerness and with the determination to make her opinions known. Her intellectual curiosity, especially about people, leads her to put her face "right in somebody's window"; her talent allows us to look through it with her.

2. Evolution of an Artist

At this writing, at a time when Norma Fox Mazer has plans for several more books, her published work already consists of thirteen novels entirely her own, one novel co-written with Harry Mazer, one novel based on a screenplay, nineteen stories, and two poems. Author of this large body of work, Mazer is less a natural storyteller than a writer who is thoughtful about certain topics, ethical questions, and relationships, and who thoroughly enjoys the process of writing about her ideas.

One of the most consistent aspects of her work is inconsistency; that is, she is a relentless experimenter with forms. Many fiction writers publish an unpolished first novel that hints of the promise of a later, more mature style; their later books show a development of that same style. Mazer's first book, however, is a polished, first-person narrative. She abandons this form in her second book, which is third-person prose that is sometimes awkwardly written. Thus, she is likely to disregard the groundwork she has laid for her stylistic development in one book in order to try something completely different in the next. She will tailor a book's individual style to suit its subject. Yet, some elements of the idiosyncratic prose forms that contribute to her personal style pervade almost all her work.

The kind of prose Mazer excels in is realistic, contemporary fiction that explores relationships among middle-class people, especially those between a woman and a girl. Lou Willett Stanek commented in 1976 on the dearth of books about such relationships, especially mother-daughter ones.[1] Mazer has gone a long way toward filling this gap; this kind of writing is her forte. She frequently discusses the concerns of intelligent, independent-minded young women who confront their problems. She does not limit herself to such topics and characters, however, and the topic of her individual works seems to determine the forms and structure of her prose.

The prose that Mazer writes best is typified in some of her short stories, a novel written in the middle of her career, and in her recent novel, *Three Sisters*. Her most mature style is fast-paced, economical prose that both gets inside her characters' heads and adeptly uses dialogue to move the action along, yet she is an artist and a crafter of words and stories who does not settle down to perfect one style or progress from book to book in a conventional way.

In *I, Trissy*, Mazer's first novel, she uses a variety of literary devices to create a vivid character, Trissy Beers, who at age eleven constantly gets into trouble and feels that life is unfair to her. She's a fresh girl by anyone's standards, talking back to teachers and parents, but she is also perceptive, sensitive, and a talented writer. In the course of the novel she comes to terms with her parents' separation, finally acknowledging what she had not wanted to believe at first. She tells herself, "Open your eyes."

It is hard to draw many conclusions about Mazer's prose style from her first novel; it is easy to see that she is interested in experimenting with technique. The entire book is written on Trissy's typewriter. There are dramatic scenes, set up like scenes from a play; stories Trissy concocts; lists; compositions written for school; imaginary newspaper articles; and finally, a diary entry. The entire book reads like a diary or journal, as Trissy is recording her thoughts on a typewriter. Later in the 1970s, so many young adult protagonists told their stories through letters or diaries that the device became trite.[2] Indeed, during those later years the technique became so common that a reviewer would pick up a new book, recognize the diary form, and just hope for something special, something with a little depth.

In *I, Trissy*, which may have set an example for later writers

of the many journal-like or epistolary novels, readers do find
depth; they find a fine story, a humorous, touching one; a protagonist to care about; and a fast-paced, lively reading experience.
The many fresh and varied forms make for enjoyable reading,
and the facsimile pages of double-spaced typing add to the book's
tone. In most of her books Mazer employs some of the literary
forms she uses in *I, Trissy*, but only in this first novel are the
forms used exclusively, without the explication of third- or first-
person narrative.

An example of the immediacy, the humor, and the success of
the style Mazer uses in this novel is Trissy's description of a tense
moment. Trissy, her brother Mitch, her mother, and her mother's
boyfriend are having Mitch's birthday dinner when Trissy makes
up her mind to telephone her father. She wants him back in the
family circle so badly that she lies, telling her father that Mitch
is crying for him. Then she returns to the table, dreading the
consequence of what she has done:

> My stomach had been growling and working ever since I made
> the phone call. Suddenly I burped. It was very loud, like this
> UUURRRP and came so fast I didn't have time to cover my
> mouth.
>   Mom gave me a freezing what-horrible-manners look. Mitch
> snickered in a superior way even though he burps all the time
> himself, and MUCH louder and more vulgar than I could hope
> to be.

The depth of character that Mazer reveals through her use of
unusual forms can be seen in a passage about Trissy and her
mother. This is the first of the many vivid mother-daughter relationships found in Mazer's novels. Trissy's mother finds a spirited memo Trissy has written, "MEMO TO MY MOTHER," which lists
Trissy's suggestions "to . . . increase your chances of persuading
my father to come live with us again," a notion Trissy can't, at
this point, imagine that her mother would not embrace. Some of
the tips included are to look interested when her husband tells
stories, to practice acting like a girlfriend's mother ("a real

MOTHER"), who is pretty, sweet, and loving, and to "get sweeter."
Trissy's account of the emotion-charged exchange describes Mrs.
Beers's fury when she reads it. Trissy objects to her mother having
read it:

> "My desk is private. You had no business snooping—"
> WHAM! She caught me across the face. "Don't you call me
> a snoop besides everything else, Trissy Beers." Her voice was
> high and shaking. My cheek stung, and I wanted to cry, but I
> hated her so much I grinned instead.

Trissy is a vivid, immediate character; readers come to know
her well, to watch her logic develop as she tries to control herself,
and when she fails to do so. One can see in a passage like this
that Mazer has sympathy for the mother as well as for the daughter; the mother is no cardboard character, but a person who is
obviously hurt by what Trissy has done; hence her voice is "high
and shaking."

The techniques used captivate readers, lend sympathy to the
protagonist, and make the book a success. One does not, however,
come away from the book with any sense of Mazer's competence
as a prose writer. If her style was, at this point in her development,
amateurish, or awkward, the child's voice used throughout the
novel would mask its shortcomings.

Mazer's next book, *A Figure of Speech,* has only one break from
conventional narrative in it: a list of "assets" and "liabilities" that
the protagonist, thirteen-year-old Jenny, assigns to herself. In-
terestingly, Mazer re-uses in the list a complaint that Trissy made
in *I, Trissy:* Jenny points out that she is not liked as much by
her parents as the other children in the family are. The rest of
the book consists of third-person narrative, from Jenny's point of
view, for the most part; the narrative is sometimes told from her
grandfather's point of view.

The novel is a moving, powerful story of the relationship between Jenny Pennoyer, an unplanned, "unwanted" child, and her
eighty-three-year-old grandfather, Carl Pennoyer, who essen-

tially raised her. Carl's wife died the year Jenny was born, and as the baby came into the hectic, cramped, middle-class Pennoyer household, a symbiotic relationship grew up between the old man and his grandchild. When the mother was overwhelmed by her chores, Carl would take baby Jenny away from the hubbub and care for her.

The book opens when Jenny's older brother Vince brings home his bride, and the couple wants—and gets—the basement apartment that is Grandpa's home. The old man fares badly after he is turned out of his apartment to share a bedroom with his other grandson, prompting Jenny's parents to decide to place him in a nursing home against his wishes. Jenny, "hot as a firecracker," is a child powerless to win the fight against her family to stop these changes in her beloved grandfather's life. She accepts, finally, that Grandpa will lose his basement apartment, but when Jenny is powerless to prevent the second catastrophe, the decision to place Grandpa in a nursing home against his will, she unleashes her fury by throwing herself down on the ground in frustration. It is an easy decision for Jenny to run away from home when her grandfather, feeling unwanted and wishing to return to a farm where he used to live, leaves the family forever.

On the whole, the book is well written. It is obvious that, as Mazar has mentioned, it was carefully planned. It is, as critic Jill Paton Walsh says, written in a "quiet, remorselessly realistic style."[3] *A Figure of Speech* is a carefully structured novel. One can see the climax, the denouement as clearly as if they were elements of a sentence being parsed. Jenny and Carl have found the old farm with its dilapidated house. After they've struggled to live there together for a few days, isolated from other people, a thunderstorm makes the run-down house even more unpleasant, as the rain leaks in. The next morning, in the climactic scene, Jenny discovers her grandfather, outside, dead. She speaks to his lifeless body, covers him with flowers, and vainly tries to dig a grave for him before she gives up and leaves to get help. The last chapter of the book serves as a classic denouement, revealing the outcome of Jenny's further actions, explaining the cause of Carl's death and the manner in which Jenny's family is able to dismiss the terrible circumstances of his death. It is Mazer's most traditional novel.

There are some awkwardnesses, some flaws; the strength of the narrative is somewhat diluted by the switching from Jenny to Carl Pennoyer, for instance. Mazer has a tendency, more than do other authors of young adult literature, to present the thoughts of adults—often of mothers, but in this case, of Grandfather Pennoyer—instead of just the thoughts of the teenage protagonists. The power of the narrative is weakened because the focus on Jenny's thoughts and concerns is neglected. Instead of learning of Carl's feelings through Jenny, we are distracted from Jenny's feelings by the change in narrator.

There are two scenes in which the plot is far-fetched. One occurs at the height of the campaign to oust Grandfather Pennoyer from his apartment: A noisy party is taking place in the room above him, and when he bursts into it, the teenage participants jeer at him, carry on as if they are drunken adults, and actually ram him into the wall. This behavior is not credible because Mazer has shown the family members to be fairly reasonable, decent people, despite not being sensitive and thoughtful like Jenny. The teenagers' behavior more closely resembles criminal acts committed by a street gang, particularly when the boys escalate the abuse beyond verbal ridicule and resort to being physically rough with the old man.

Another unlikely act of cruelty toward the grandfather occurs when Jenny's mother gives away all of his possessions, including an old Victrola and a collection of 78 RPM recordings, while Grandpa is ill and doesn't know what is going on. Would the woman truly be so cruel? She has never been portrayed as the sort of malicious character who might be capable of this act. Mazer has presented her as a woman who tells Jenny it is "no picnic" living with the old man; she must work harder at household chores because of him, she must tolerate his tedious storytelling, and she holds Jenny with "pleading eyes" that beg her to understand her point of view. Acts like roughing up Carl and discarding his prize possessions seem unnecessarily exaggerated extensions of the rudeness the other family members show Grandpa, rudeness that Jenny and readers find appalling enough.

The strongest aspects of the book are Jenny's strong character, the dominant theme of hypocrisy, the moving relationship between Jenny and her grandfather, and the powerful, unflinchingly realistic climax of the novel. Jenny's character is made vivid through skillfully written passages that reveal her strong personality. There is a "deep, underlying irritation" between her and her mother, which she had realized at the age of eleven. She tried being "sweet and good" but found it a terrific strain; nothing she tried could change their relationship. The theme of hypocrisy pervades the book. Jenny confronts her parents at dinner, questioning why they tell her to respect her elders, but don't treat her grandfather respectfully. And even after Carl is dead, she overhears her parents speaking fondly of Carl, ignoring the truth, and the hypocrisy makes her run out of the house. The lovely relationship between Carl and his grandchild is made clear from both Jenny's eagerness to rise at 6 A.M. to go downstairs to spend time with Carl before school, and from Carl's realization that Jenny is the reason he gets out of bed each morning.

A Figure of Speech affords our first example of Mazer's third-person, descriptive style. The care she takes with these passages demonstrates her ability to write such prose at this stage in her development. An example of this rich prose is the death imagery that begins the chapter in which Grandfather dies: Mazer uses words and phrases like "clammy," "chill," "grass stiff with silver frost," "deep hush," and "cold ground." Her later books, however, largely eschew descriptive prose and concentrate on techniques that get her closer to her characters' thoughts.

Mazer's third book is utterly different from either of the books that came before it. It is ambitious and complicated; there are several ways to categorize it. *Saturday, the Twelfth of October* is a book of "biological realism,"[4] that is, it discusses the menarche; it is a fantasy that presents an entire fictitious matriarchal society; and it is a time-travel novel.

The book came out in 1975, when there was a profusion of stories about girls going through puberty; many authors seemed to be following the lead of Judy Blume, who discussed menstruation in her popular 1970 novel, *Are You There, God? It's Me, Margaret.* Many young adult books published at that time that featured a teenage girl included a scene of "biological realism," as one reviewer commented, in "stories that do not need it."[5] The seemingly obligatory scenes were frequently whimsically added to an unrelated story, and they were beginning to be tiresome. In *Saturday, the Twelfth of October,* however, the subject is crucial to the book.

The menarche is important to the novel because Mazer has created in her fantasy novel an entire culture in which the menarche plays an important part. The details of the fictitious, prehistoric society are so believable that one might expect to pick up *The Golden Bough,* the seminal book on comparative religion and mythology, and find Mazer's society described there. Her matriarchal world includes its own religion, folklore, names, speech, customs, and rituals of birth, death, and coming of age. Zan Ford, the protagonist of *Saturday,* wishes, alone, for her own menarche in contemporary American society, when the event is considered unmentionable. Then she is thrown back in time to a culture where, she discovers with delight, a girl's coming of age is a joyous occasion. There is a great deal of depth to Mazer's matriarchal culture, with carefully thought-out explanations of not only the day-to-day workings of the society, but the customs of mourning and burial, the procedure of healing the sick, and the inclusion of evil spirits as well as a higher god. The book attempts so much and achieves so much that, in fact, it is the kind of book least well served by the two-hundred-word reviews that appear in review journals in the field of children's and young adult literature.

Last, but not least, the novel is a time-travel fantasy. Zan, a contemporary fourteen-year-old in an agitated state of mind, runs to a spot in a park and finds herself thrown back to prehistoric times. She stays with the tribal people for almost a year, but on her return to modern-day civilization, she finds that she has been gone for only a day. The portrayal of another time period is successful, but the portrayal of the back-and-forth journeys themselves is less so. Mazer describes traveling through time in terms of elemental changes such as sounds Zan hears and sensations she experiences: "Then a storm of darkness descended on her, wings of darkness spinning and tossing her in a blur of silver and black." The lack of precision in the description of what exactly is happening may enhance the mysterious effect of the process, but the vagueness is unsatisfying. In this case, Mazer has tried for something a little different and failed.

The scope of *Saturday* is radically different from Mazer's two previous books. From writing about the small cast of characters in *I, Trissy,* with a time span of a few weeks, Mazer has gone on to write a novel about an entire society. Its time frame spans a year in the past as well as a day in the present. The best aspect of the book is the society that Mazer creates. Zan's reactions to the strange, gentle, nonviolent people range from her initial confusion to fascination and delight with them. Her insights are recognized by readers, who are afforded the opportunity to gain perspective on their own society by comparing Zan's world to theirs.

The most difficult problem the book has is its point of view. Mazer changes the point of view from one character to another, a technique not entirely satisfactorily employed in *A Figure of Speech*. The first change in the point of view is from Zan to her brother Ivan. Perhaps Mazer wants her readers to understand why Ivan steals Zan's diary, an action that distresses Zan greatly; yet it is not necessary for readers to feel sympathy for Ivan, and the change of point of view attenuates the strength of the narrative.

Later, the point of view is switched for an entire chapter to Sonte, a girl Zan's age who, along with the boy Farwe, were the first of the tribal people to see Zan when she appeared in their world. The following chapter is from Zan's point of view, but the next is from Farwe's. The perspective wanders so far afield that Zan is quite lost from the reader's view at times. This is unfortunate, because one of Mazer's strengths throughout her works is a close identification with her readers; in her later work Mazer never moves so far away from her main character; here the pace of *Saturday* is weakened. *Saturday* is the only one of the Mazer's books to contain long descriptive passages, but it is also her only book to have such a broad scope. The story will interest only readers who do not mind the descriptive passages needed to make the world and its many characters understandable. The descriptions are sometimes clumsily written, as when Zan recovers from her time-travel trip. "She lay on the ground, crumpled, shaking, bones scraped raw," the text reads. It is clear that the experience has been terrifying, but it is not clear what has actually happened to Zan's body. Gradually it "knit itself together" and, as she waits, "stunning, needle-like flashes of black and silver pierced her skull." How could Zan discern the colors of "flashes" if they are literally piercing her skull? They could seem to pierce her skull, but this description and others that detail her time travel are confusing and lack sense, as, for example, "Her mind sank and drowned."

There is also a dearth of dialogue, and dialogue that quickens the pace of the book's action is usually one of Mazer's strengths as a writer; it is a technique she handled well in *A Figure of Speech*. The style of *Saturday* is atypical of Mazer. The complexity and scope of her subject and her interest in the details of the society she has created determined that she tell this story differently from Trissy's story, or from Karen's story in her most recent book, *Three Sisters*.

Mazer is ever the experimenter, and while she is not successful when she switches the point of view as she does, she does succeed in employing a stream-of-consciousness technique in *Saturday*. She uses it effectively to convey Zan's bewildered state of mind as, alone, she blunders through the forest:

> Trees. Everywhere, trees. Enormous, overwhelming, trunks rising straight into the air, huge columns, or twisting grotesquely. Surrounded on all sides by trees . . . living trees . . . dying trees . . . dead trees . . .

The repetition of the word *trees* highlights the monotony of her surroundings as Zan seeks other people. The technique is a more intense version of Zan's third-person, omniscient narrative, in which most of the book is told: "She had left the knife. . . . It had brought so much grief, terror, pain already! But what else could she have done?"

Mazer's next book was a collection of short stories, *Dear Bill, Remember Me? And Other Stories.* Mazer told her editor she'd like to write a book of short stories, and though he replied that such collections were "shelf-sitters," he said to go ahead because maybe it was time for more short stories to be published. The result, including the stories in her second volume, *Summer Girls, Love Boys and Other Short Stories,* is some of the best work Mazer has done. The stories in *Dear Bill* are told from a wide variety of points of view, as Mazer's novels are. First-person accounts are used: straightforwardly, in "Chocolate Pudding," and in more varied ways in other stories. Two are told in the form of letters ("Dear Bill, Remember Me?" and "Avie Loves Ric Forever"); one is an oral history transcription ("Carmella, Adelina, and Florry"); and one first-person account records one side of a series of conversations between a girl and her school psychologist.

As in her novels, Mazer uses many forms and literary devices to tell her stories. She is frequently at the height of her stylistic powers in the stories. "Dear Bill . . .," with its compact, poignant tale seamlessly told; "Guess Whose Friendly Hands," told in the confines of a dying girl's sickroom; and "I, Hungry Hannah Cassandra Glen . . . ," with its razor-sharp realism and its perfectly crafted, fast pace shine as examples of Mazer's finest work. It seems reasonable to assume that her years of writing short fiction pieces for magazines honed her ability to write stories.

The Solid Gold Kid, which was published in 1977, exhibits little of Mazer's style as exemplified in her other fiction, and is useless as an example of her progress as a writer. She and Harry Mazer decided to collaborate on a book, and this is the result. It is a fast-paced, suspenseful survival novel with a far-fetched plot. Derek, the son of a millionaire, is kidnapped from school, but the kidnappers also take along the four young people who are hitching a ride with him. Readers witness the five being kidnapped, threatened, and imprisoned. They are deprived of food and water, and one character's pet is killed; the Mazers don't actually kill off a person. The group seems calculatedly varied, allowing conflicts to develop among the strange bedfellows. There is one rich boy, one black boy, one bigot, one girl who cries and shows her weakness, and one strong, more independent girl, the romantic interest of the rich boy. The two criminals are never very convincing. While readers may recognize some hallmarks of Norma Fox Mazer's style (a letter appears in the text, from Derek's sister, and Derek's thoughts are presented in a stream-of-consciousness technique: "Prodded forward. Stumbling. Prodded forward again. My arm twisted behind my back "), this co-written adventure novel is not really the work of either author.

Up in Seth's Room, which closely followed *The Solid Gold Kid,* is a book that Mazer wrote in order to address a specific topic: sexuality among teenagers. The book's protagonist is fifteen-year-old Finn Rousseau. Finn's older sister Maggie has been living with her boyfriend Jim for about a year, and relations between the couple and the Rousseaus are so strained that Finn's father hangs up on Maggie when she calls home. Finn's friend Vida is a sexually active girl who is trying to push Finn into dating Jerry, a boy at school, whom Finn knows will expect that she go to bed with him. Finn is not attracted to Jerry, but she is immediately attracted to Seth, Jim's younger brother. Finn's parents forbid Finn to see Seth because he is four years older than she is and because he is Jim's brother. Finn finds irony in this situation because she knows that the boy from school whom her parents would approve of would be more of a threat to her virginity than Seth.

Though Mazer set out to write the book about a certain external subject, the novel is none the weaker for it. Mazer couldn't be closer to her protagonist than she is in *Up in Seth's Room,* with the authentic voice of Finn. In this novel Mazer hits her stride. Finn is pressured by everyone, by her best friend (to go out with Jerry), by her parents (to drop Seth), by, finally, Seth (to sleep with him); but Finn is an independent-minded, strong character who faces her problems and the pressures put upon her and works them out, making a few concessions to her parents, but none to her integrity.

The book has a strong, mature style, with just a few awkward moments. As in *Saturday, the Twelfth of October,* Mazer's descriptions do not always succeed in making the thought processes of her characters understandable to the reader. This lack of clarity is evident as Mazer describes Finn and Seth embracing intimately (they have taken off their clothes), but not having intercourse; Finn has decided that she is not ready for that, and Seth has accepted her decision:

> He turned away. He was singing. He always sang. She had her arms around him, her face pressed against his back. She floated in golden circles, spinning higher and higher, the circles narrowing and golden, dazzling.

Not only do the sentences "He was singing. He always sang," strike an odd note—the reader was never before given to understand that Seth sings after he has a sexual climax—but the vagueness of the passage is both unsatisfying and inconsistent with the realistic description in the rest of the book.

Perhaps it is this scene that prompted some negative criticism of the book when it was published. Patty Campbell observed in the *Wilson Library Bulletin* that Finn "accepts every other form of intimacy with cheerful enthusiasm, but protects her technical virginity with hysterical zeal."[6] The phrase "hysterical zeal" misinterprets Finn's concerns; rather, she is strong and resolved to making her own decisions, not being pressured by anyone to have sex too soon, or even to date someone she doesn't like.

Like Campbell, *Kirkus Reviews* described Finn and Seth's manner of lovemaking as "what might well be seen as a ludicrous solution in these days when technical virginity has pretty much lost its cachet."[7] Again, this kind of assessment misses Mazer's point: She doesn't have Finn remain a virgin for the sake of a definition of morality; she is championing the right of a teenage girl to choose, for herself, what is right for her at the right time in her life, and Finn, although ready for a degree of sexual intimacy, is not ready for intercourse.

Another criticism made of the book, however, is apt. Critics make a valid point that Seth's departure for another part of the country at the book's end puts a neat end to the relationship. Were fifteen-year-old Finn and nineteen-year-old Seth to continue their romance, one wonders if Finn would, finally, give in to Seth's wishes over her own. However, Mazer is certainly not avoiding the portrayal of a full sexual relationship between teenagers; Finn's best friend Vida is having sex with her boyfriend.

This novel has some other weaknesses, such as occasional contrived dialogue. Mazer presents an exchange between Finn and a girl named Nancy, attempting to show how the girl "was always trying to get under Finn's skin." A gym teacher complains that the girls in the "physical ed" class are not making any effort. Finn calls out that they might be called the "physical dead" class. Nancy says to Finn, "A very witty remark. Where'd you hear it?" When Finn tells Nancy she's made it up, Nancy smiles "disbelievingly." The remark is not witty enough to provoke this exchange: it seems unlikely that Nancy would ask the source of such a remark, so the conversation seems forced. The book has a strange epigraph, too ("First he taught her. Then she taught him. It was like a race where they passed the baton from one to the other. Then they took it together and ran."), that is reminiscent of the kind of enticing copy that usually appears on the covers of mass-market paperback novels.

In most of the book, however, Mazer excels in capturing the essence of her protagonist and presenting her thoughts and feelings with utmost immediacy to her readers. For example, after her parents have forbidden her to see Seth, Finn and her mother have a futile conversation. Her mother tells her she wants to talk to her, and to get in the car.

Finn put her books on the seat between her and her mother. She looked out the window. If her mother wanted to talk, let her talk. She didn't have anything to say.

"Look," her mother said. . . . "I'm older and I look at things differently. I have—well, call it wisdom, you don't have."

Like hell I'll call it wisdom. Finn stared out the frosty window.

"Finn, are you listening?" Finn didn't turn her head.

Finn's mother recounts a time when she spanked Finn, as a baby, for running into the road. She is trying to show her that she taught Finn something about a dangerous thing.

> "Do you understand? I was acting for your own good."
>   Shut up, Finn thought, just shut up and don't ever talk to me again.

Later, when Maggie and Finn clash, Finn manages, by her attitude and by her conversation with her older sister, to demand Maggie's respect. She evaluates the meeting afterwards: "Maggie had dropped her older-sister pose at the end and just spoken to Finn like another person. Good, Finn thought. Good!" Mazer's trademark narrative embellishments appear in the book: As Finn sits in the library, she imagines the text of a newspaper article as she daydreams; she writes in a notebook, playing with words and letting her mind wander; and she thinks up newspaper headlines about her situation: *"Flash . . .* 19-YEAR-OLD BROTHER OF SISTER'S LIVE-IN BOYFRIEND ASKS FOR DATE. OUTRAGED MOTHER STRANGLES DAUGHTER." Though *A Figure of Speech* and *I, Trissy* were fine stylistic achievements, in *Up in Seth's Room* Mazer has become more adept at revealing the thoughts and feelings of her protagonist. She has tuned her writing style to make Finn's crucial problems and triumphant nature come alive, and she has focused the point of view solely on Finn, which makes the narrative voice stronger than in *A Figure of Speech* or *Saturday*.

Mazer's next novel is *Mrs. Fish, Ape, and Me, the Dump Queen*. The whimsical, lengthy title, typical of many children's and young adult book titles, serves to emphasize the odd trio that is the book's subject.

Joyce is ostracized at school because Old Dad (also called "Ape" because of his appearance), her guardian and uncle, runs the county dump. Joyce's classmates call her "The Dump Queen" and fill her school desk with garbage. Joyce gets along well with her gruff, stubborn uncle and accepts her life the way it is, having learned not to show her feelings to the children who torment her. She has one fantasy: that some mistake was made about her mother's death in a car crash, and that her mother will return to her.

This excellent book is for readers aged eight to twelve, younger than Mazer's usual young adult audience, and the heroine is elementary-school-age. Joyce is an outsider, and Mazer captures that quality extremely well. Joyce is accustomed to the way she is treated by other children, and yet she can be hurt; she still remains open to possible friendship. She is an admirable character who knows what is important, who is respectful of her skeptical Old Dad but who is strong enough to lead him to open up to a new person in both of their lives—Mrs. Fish, the eccentric, even outlandish custodian of Joyce's school.

The entire novel is told in a strong, first-person narrative, a point of view that Mazer has not used since *Dear Bill, Remember Me?* She does not waste words; the result is a direct, compelling reading experience. The narrative voice allows readers to feel close to Joyce, to detect her perception and sensitivity. For instance, in one passage Joyce is confronted by Lacey, a new girl in their school. A friendship has been blossoming between the two, until their classmates tell Lacey that Joyce lives in a dump, that she is taboo. Their conversation is interspersed with Joyce's brief commentary: "The softer her voice got, the louder mine got"; and "I thought maybe I was close to crying, so I made mean eyes. . . ." Mazer shows, in a child's wording, how Joyce defends herself against being hurt. Readers also care so much about this winning character that they want to turn the pages quickly; one of the chapter titles is "What Are We Going To Do?"—and readers share Joyce's anxiety at that point.

The dialogue is also convincing. Mazer duplicates the speech and presents the personality of Old Dad here as well as she brought Grandpa to life in *A Figure of Speech*. His gruff, terse conversation is consistently believable. Conversations with teachers, classmates, and Mrs. Fish are done equally well. For example, when the other children in the classroom are being cruel to Joyce, the dialogue is authentic, with several children joining in. Their comments are smoothly interspersed with matter-of-fact observation, which make the comments more powerful in contrast, and which also reinforce Joyce's characterization as both sensitive and brave as she attempts to ignore the children's cruelty.

Mazer switches effortlessly back to her younger audience, the audience of *I, Trissy,* with this novel; she addresses the younger age group so well that it is easy to forget that she writes primarily for young adults. Mazer's young protagonists are quite different from her fifteen-year-old heroines; rather than being concerned with romantic relationships, the younger characters are concerned with such subjects as having and losing a best friend. Trissy temporarily loses her friend Steffi in *I, Trissy,* and Joyce finds, loses, and regains the friendship of Lacey in *Mrs. Fish.*

Mrs. Fish is a poignant, serious book that explores the pain of being an outsider and allows us to come to know a lovable character; and the happy ending, unconventional because Mrs. Fish and Old Dad are going to live together, though unmarried, is quite welcome.

Taking Terri Mueller, published in 1981, is a novel on the subject of a contemporary topic: parental kidnapping. Thirteen-year-old Terri, who lives a nomadic life with her father, begins to ask discomfiting questions about her mother's death, which Terri understands took place when she was four. The truth, she eventually finds, is that her father kidnapped her after he lost custody of his child. Terri, a strong character, overhears a puzzling conversation and makes persistent efforts to discover the truth, courageously challenging her stubborn father. The novel, which won an Edgar Allan Poe Award for best juvenile mystery, is an unconventional mystery, but a suspenseful story. It is written almost cinematically: Chapters recall movie scenes, with descriptions of places, the pace, and the drama of events lending themselves to film treatment. Terri's curiosity leads her relentlessly to her mother, and one particularly suspenseful moment occurs as she makes the phone call in which she speaks with her mother for the first time since she was kidnapped.

The prose in *Taking Terri* is strong, with well-written dialogue, and Terri's thoughts are convincingly presented. When she first confronts her father with the news that she has overheard information, she puts a question forth with difficulty. The description of her father's bewilderment and his stalling before making a reply is faithfully recorded, interspersed with realistic dialogue. We are privy to Terri's thoughts as she realizes that she must find out the truth about her mother: *"I want answers,"* she says out loud, alone in their apartment.

Most of the book is told from Terri's point of view, but once again its viewpoint switches to her father in one chapter and even to Terri's mother, after Terri has arrived to become reacquainted with her, taking the reader away from Terri.

Mazer's by-now-familiar letters and journal entries pop up in *Taking Terri,* adding variety to the story, and she also uses a new technique in this book. Sitting in school one day, Terri relives the events of the previous day, including a conversation that readers are eager to hear. It is the conversation between Terri and her father after Terri has confronted him with her knowledge that he divorced her mother. In this conversation Terri and the reader learn the truth about her kidnapping. Terri's thoughts show how unimportant school events are in comparison with what she is reacting to in her personal life, in addition to revealing events in an original and compelling manner. Similarly, when Terri is out with her friend Shaundra, she is planning how to get into a private box of her father's to get the information she seeks, rather than concentrating on Shaundra:

> "Let's do something. What should we do?"
> "I don't know, what do you want to do?" Terri said. Could she have a key made? In stories people were always making wax impressions of keys.
> "Let's go to the drugstore and look at magazines."
> "Okay." Or else they had sensitive fingers that knew how to make locks open with a touch.

After Terri takes in the information that her mother is alive, Mazer likens her feelings to those of someone who has been in an accident. Mazer describes this lack of feeling, "frozen nerves," until "later, much later . . . you find the bruises, and discover that you ache everywhere." This use of the second person is yet another narrative device in *Taking Terri*. Mazer has mixed many of the techniques she has used previously and added some intriguing new ones.

When We First Met, her eighth novel, may have a familiar air to readers for several reasons. First, the book's protagonist is Jenny Pennoyer, of *A Figure of Speech*, who is now seventeen. Second, the novel has a Romeo and Juliet plot, which Mazer exploits well for her purposes. Third, the story recalls a notion raised in *Taking Terri Mueller*. At the opening of the book we learn that Gail, Jenny's sister, has been dead for two years, the victim of a car accident in which the driver had been drinking. This contemporary, controversial subject is discussed in the book, but the story is never overwhelmed by the topical nature of drunken driving; instead, Mazer explores the effects the accident has had on all of the book's characters.

Jenny falls in love at first sight with a golden-haired boy at school; they smile and exchange a few words, obviously "clicking"; Jenny wonders, "Was this the unnameable 'it' for which she had been waiting so long?" But feckless Jenny soon discovers that Robin, the new light of her life, is the son of Nell Montana, the drunken driver who killed her sister Gail. Jenny, like Juliet, experiences "My only love sprung from my only hate! Too early seen unknown, and known too late!"

The Shakespearian plot is not strictly followed: there is no missed message and there are no deaths (unlike another modern Romeo and Juliet tale, *West Side Story*). But the name "Montana" is close to "Montague"; Jenny's friend Rhoda points out that Robin and Jenny's initials are the same as the star-crossed lovers; and there is some "what's in a name" banter. The similarity that the author concentrates on is a situation like the one in *Up in Seth's Room:* The protagonist is seeing a forbidden boy. Curiously, Mazer has also based this novel on an idea mentioned in another: In *Taking Terri*, Terri speculates on the whereabouts of the driver who supposedly killed her mother in a car accident: "Where was he now? What if she met him someday and knew he was the one who had killed her mother?" The plot of *When We First Met* is, therefore, both familiar and intriguing.

The style is solid Mazer, though it is inconsistent and contains both brilliant and awkward prose. Many of the narrative devices that Mazer's readers have come to expect are present: newspaper articles, letters, thoughts specified in italics, and abbreviated sentences that convey information and move the action quickly. There is even an amusing dialogue between Jenny and Rob that Jenny imagines in a daydream, complete with stage directions. Mazer once again deviates from the point of view of the protagonist to show adults' thoughts, but here the technique is not as jolting to readers as are the sections of adults' points of view in previous books. This is because parents' actions are more crucial to the plot of *When We First Met* than they are in other books. The thoughts of the parents of Robin and Jenny are brought into focus so that readers can understand the effects of Gail's death on all, and can evaluate Jenny's reactions and decisions to events within the story.

The prose is occasionally reminiscent of a mass-market paperback romance, weighty and overly dramatic; when Jenny realizes she has sent Rob away from her, "Only then . . . did she fully understand what she had done." Jenny has ended a relationship "beyond words, beyond either words or silence." She concludes: "They had made their love together. She alone had destroyed it." This triteness is tempered by the high degree of sophistication that Mazer attains in setting up situations, moving the action, and conveying a wealth of information and feeling in a bit of dialogue. She does this with terrific economy of words when a party is mentioned, discussed, and under way in a trice. A short sentence introduces Rhoda's intent to have a party. When Jenny is reluctant to come, Rhoda urges her to, and the next paragraph deftly places them at Rhoda's on the night of the party. Mazer's sure hand as a writer of contemporary realistic young adult fiction is obvious here; she is a long way from relying on the lengthy descriptions of *Saturday*.

Someone to Love centers on the longing to be part of a couple, a frequent minor theme in Mazer's previous novels. Strong, independent Nina is at nineteen the eldest of all Mazer's protagonists. Nina is away from home, living with two other girls, and lonely for a boyfriend when she meets Mitch (Mitch Beers, borrowed from *I, Trissy*, a few years older). The book chronicles their love affair from infatuation to blissful cohabitation to separation, after both Nina and Mitch have had sex with other people. Nina's encounter was a spontaneous lovemaking session with Nicholas Lehman, a college professor she works for.

When Nina finally moves out, convinced she's made a mistake, that she didn't know Mitch well enough to live with him, Mitch reacts to her disappointment: "Nobody knows anybody, not really, Nina. This is a lonely world. Haven't you figured that one out yet?" Nina also listens to her sister Nancy, who describes life as a house that has a different party going on in every room, all of which she wants to go to. Yet Nina draws her own conclusion: Her affair with Mitch was not "the real thing," but true love does exist nevertheless.

The plot of *Someone to Love* is not as intriguing as those of Mazer's other novels; the most vital elements of the story are the conversations between Nina and her strikingly different sister. This is not surprising, considering Mazer's penchant for capturing sisters' relationships well. Nina is a character largely seen as a partner in a relationship, and perhaps this is why the book is not so vital as Mazer's other books, which treat romance as a secondary concern of characters and concentrate more on the individual.

The book has the clear tone of a college campus on a Saturday afternoon, with a bright blue sky, and the telling is sure and smooth. Mazer is particularly adept in this novel at interspersing action with the staccato thoughts of her protagonist. For instance, Nina returns to school and to Mitch, after a vacation, full of stories to tell him, but he does not respond. She thinks: "Each time, a shock . . . something was wrong." She hangs on his arm. "Mitch allowed her to hang there. *That* was it. He *allowed* it."

The style does falter during the sexual encounter between Nina and her college professor when, as in *Saturday* and in *Up in Seth's Room,* the description briefly becomes too vague to explain what exactly is happening. The professor is holding her, comforting her, she feels, about the death of her pet cat. She burrows into him, to be "close and comforted." Then the sexual encounter is described as the two "falling" on the rug, "close, close, close"; only this sentence portrays the act: "She heard someone crying, little mewing sounds, oh, oh, oh, it was her. . . . And all this was mixed with her tears." Other authors could present a sexual scene similarly without the ambiguity being noticed, but Mazer describes every other word and act in the rest of the book so realistically that her vagueness here appears equivocal.

Throughout most of the novel, however, the stylistic devices Mazer employs make Nina a vivid character. One particularly rich narrative device is the reproduction of one of Nina's school papers, in which she analyzes a short story. The theme of the story concerns just letting things happen versus not allowing one's self to be defeated, and Nina weaves into her analysis some connections between her own life and this theme. Another successful stylistic device Mazer uses here is demonstrated in her thoughts as she and Mitch climb onto a seesaw at a playground: "Odd how you felt things in layers. Laughter, eating an ice cream, bobbing like a kid on a seesaw—all on one layer. On another layer, chewing over that sudden meeting with Nicholas Lehman." Here is another instance of Mazer's fine melding of her protagonists' mundane surroundings and everyday activities with the crucial concerns that are sometimes hidden in their thoughts.

Pete Greenwood of *Downtown* is only the second male protagonist to appear in one of Mazer's novels, after Derek of *The Solid Gold Kid*. In *Downtown* sixteen-year-old Pete lives with his uncle, because when he was a small child, his political activist parents had to go underground after they accidentally killed two people while bombing a laboratory. Pete receives sporadic letters from his parents and lives in fear that his true identity will be found out. The book does not exhibit much change in Mazer's style; although she excels at writing about girls, Pete is equally likable and believable. His narrative is unique among Mazer's narrative voices because it contains more humor than do the narratives of female protagonists. He recalls a girl in elementary school who demanded a bag of marbles from him for a look at her navel: "Hot stuff for fifth grade." Self-deprecatingly, he remembers his overly polite, nervous stammering in the presence of a girl he idolizes: "I all but bent from the waist."

Another of Mazer's books that does not exhibit great stylistic development is *Supergirl,* a 1984 novelization of a screenplay. Though it proves little about her style, it demonstrates that she can write to order competently. It is interesting to find techniques she uses in other novels in the writing style, such as ellipses to communicate a character's thoughts. The book is not one that Mazer's fans need to seek out; it is a different sort of novel that does not explore the themes that interest Mazer and would be of more interest to those who see the movie *Supergirl* than to the readers of *Dear Bill, Remember Me?*

From Mazer's foray into a boy's perspective on what is a complicated story of secrets and politics in *Downtown,* she comes back to familiar ground in her recent novel, the triumphant *Three Sisters*. It is a story with familiar Mazer themes and situations, and exceptionally strong characterization featuring the kind of protagonist whom she portrays most vividly.

Karen, at fifteen, is the youngest of three sisters. Liz, twenty-one, is a beauty and a poet. Tobi, eighteen, is intense and athletic. Karen mourns the breakup of the trio they used to call Katoli, for the first two letters in each of their names; Tobi and Liz seem to have outgrown her. Karen also feels overshadowed by the two older girls, so special in their own ways.

The novel's setting stays close to the family circle; it concerns Karen and her sisters and all of their boyfriends. Karen has a tough time; her boyfriend David drops her because he's ready for sex, and she isn't. In an abrupt way that hurts her very much, he tells her he'd like to break up; she would like to remain friends, and he has made this almost impossible. Then, she begins to be attracted to Liz's fiancé, Scott. This attraction isn't easy on Karen, who must rationalize constantly to herself so that she doesn't feel guilty about going after her sister's boyfriend. Scott doesn't discourage Karen's flirtation, and when Karen is finally taken seriously by her sisters, it is because she is recognized as the betrayer of one of them.

Mazer has never shown the thoughts and emotions of one of

her characters so completely as she does in *Three Sisters*. She makes Karen a totally believable, passionate, vivid character. Her style reaches its peak in this novel. One chapter can be taken as an example of the culmination of Mazer's talents as a writer of realistic fiction. The chapter begins as Karen dresses for school, in a jaunty mood. A breakfast scene is unerringly unfolded, with the kind of detail that establishes the family and their relationships solidly. Amid the eating and the presence of a television, crucial information is exchanged about Tobi and her boyfriend Jason, a man Mrs. Freed disapproves of because he is much older than Tobi. Tobi's answers to her mother's questions leave out as much information as possible, so that Mrs. Freed must drag from her the details of where she was the night before and why she didn't call home. Karen enters the conversation briefly, hoping to back Tobi up, which serves to make the whole scene a stage for Karen's reactions to family matters.

At school, Karen flirts with a boy. One can see her in her grandmother's fedora, self-confident and smiling. " 'Hiii,' " she says. She teases her boyfriend David, though they've had a fight recently. Interspersed with the dialogue is sparse narrative, from Karen's point of view, that moves the action briskly and smoothly and that richly builds Karen's character. For example, she tries to engage David in conversation; when he only answers, "Mmm," the narrative describes his dark mood: "Davey glowered. Roar. Roar. The lion in his den." The chapter ends with Karen and her friends playing football. David has been trying to avoid Karen, but he finally tells her what he wants to say at a most absurd moment, after she tackles him and the ball pops out of his hands. He helps her up, and quickly says,

> "Karen, I've been thinking. We should stop going together."
> "What?" she said, although she'd heard him perfectly.
> "Stop going together," he repeated softly. "Okay?" he said. "Okay?"

Mazer then describes how the football play begins again, and Karen hears herself say "Okay. Okay, if that's what you want, Davey," and then she runs with the other players.

Mazer's technique does not fail to capture one nuance of Karen's character, from the way she wears her hat when she's in a great mood to the way she repeats what David has told her, though she's heard him "perfectly," when she's shocked. Karen records every complex emotion that she feels, such as the guilt she experiences when Liz discovers that Karen neglected to mention that Karen had seen Scott at his apartment a few days earlier. She avoids Liz for a few days, then wriggles "uncomfortably" when she must take a car trip with Liz. Yet Karen can't stop daydreaming about Scott, even while Liz sits next to her. Mazer's care in portraying Karen results in a character and a book that readers will not forget. Mazer uses some of her traditional untraditional narrative devices in the novel—a few words from a journal, a newspaper piece—but the strengths of the book are the dialogue and Karen's reactions to people and events.

Three Sisters shares with *I, Trissy* and *Up in Seth's Room* one of the most passionate, believable heroines in Mazer's novels. This recent novel, then, combines the subject matter she writes of best, a protagonist she describes most vividly, and a style she has perfected. Mazer is a writer who can be counted on to stretch her artistic range and to experiment with ideas and with forms; she is a writer whose curiosity about life and whose care for her individual characters lead her to write intriguingly, convincingly, and entertainingly about the concerns of young adults.

3. The Craft of the Short Story

Norma Fox Mazer is one of the few writers for young adults who has published a collection of short stories. Most collections of short stories for young people, as Donald R. Gallo points out in the preface to his *Sixteen: Short Stories by Outstanding Writers for Young Adults,* are compendiums of stories written by writers for adults, stories chosen because they have teenage characters. Young adult readers may have access to these collections, such as *Point of Departure: 19 Stories of Youth and Discovery,*[1] and *An Over-praised Season: 10 Stories of Youth,*[2] whether the books are assigned in school or found in the young adult section of a bookstore, but there exist few stories "written specifically for teen-agers by authors who specialize in writing books for young people."[3] Gallo's anthology, made up of previously unpublished stories, includes one new story by Mazer that does not appear in either of her two collections.

There are a few other collections by single authors, such as the collection by Robert Cormier, writer of powerful, disturbing novels like *The Chocolate War* that are popular with young adult readers. However, his stories in *Eight Plus One: Stories,* some reprinted from the *Saturday Evening Post,* and written in the 1960s, do not comprise a stellar collection. Rather, the book merely collects various pieces of writing that are of little interest other than to Cormier's fans, who may want to read all of his work.

Lois Ruby also published a collection of short stories written for young adults, seven stories that feature teenage protagonists and plots that include elements of young adult "problem novels." In "Found by a Lost Child," for example, a high school girl tells her boyfriend she's pregnant, then bears her pregnancy without his support when he reacts badly to the news. With the help of her mother and some friends, she gives her baby up for adoption. Several of the stories treat such crisis situations: in one, a teenager kills his father for beating his younger brother. However, Ruby's stories are dominated by their sometimes sensational plots, and do not build strong reader identification as Mazer's stories do. No other collection written by a single author for young adults is as important a contribution to young adult literature as are Norma Fox Mazer's two collections.

The stories in Mazer's *Dear Bill, Remember Me? And Other Stories* and *Summer Girls, Love Boys and Other Short Stories* generally explore personal courage and a sense of independence in their female protagonists. They concentrate on the breaking away from family, maturing, and being in love, while presenting subjects as varied as death from cancer, bad working conditions in a factory, a death caused by a drunken driver, and a mentally retarded character. The points of view are sometimes unusual and the style sometimes sophisticated, assuring a strong impact and high degree of believability. Though a few of the stories are weak, most are powerful and memorable.

In examining Mazer's short stories we first need to consider that the criteria for analyzing and judging short stories differ from those for novels. Such elements as length, development of the story, time span, and scope of characters and events must be evaluated in a different way.

In order to define what a short story is, consider the ideas of Edgar Allan Poe, who wrote, in an 1842 review of Nathaniel Hawthorne's *Twice-Told Tales*, that short prose narrative requires from a half-hour to one or two hours in its perusal so that an interruption in reading does not destroy the "true unity" of the story. He described "a certain unique or single *effect* to be wrought out," and "a sense of the fullest satisfaction" on the part of the reader because "the idea of the tale has been presented unblemished, because undisturbed; and this is an end unattainable by the novel."[4] In the nearly 150 years since Poe wrote about Hawthorne, endless variations on the American short story have been written and published. Any attempt to define the modern American short story is bound to suffer by the existence of published stories that prove to be exceptions to a definition, but I will contend that it is still a prose narrative, meant to be read at one sitting, that has a single effect upon the reader.

Mazer's stories are connected by several recurring themes; the first collection is particularly cohesive. In *Dear Bill* we have many varied pictures of girls and women breaking away from their parents, growing up, accepting difficult or unpleasant circumstances, and thriving as independent young women. In "Up on Fong Mountain" Jessie describes herself as "prickly" with her father, her sister, and BD, her boyfriend. Jessie and BD often fight, and Jessie complains that he always gets his way. She bravely stands up to him in an argument, but finally swallows her pride enough to make up with him. Jessie is strong and stands up for herself, yet she is not unreasonable. The heroine of "Peter in the Park" also finds the courage to stand up for herself. A girl raised and beloved by three women feels suffocated by their attention; she rebels by going to a "dangerous" park alone, and in the final episode of the story runs out of the house to the park in the middle of the night. On her return home she doesn't answer her relatives' demands for an explanation, knowing "she can't remain their little Zoe forever. . . . she did what she meant to do, and to tell the truth, she feels, quite simply, splendid." The masterpiece "Dear Bill, Remember Me?" reveals the devotion Kathy has held for years for an unattainable older boy, and then shows how she manages to write a restrained, proper, and mature note to him congratulating him upon his marriage.

In "Mimi the Fish" Mimi's mother is protrayed as a woman who is reliving her own past through her daughter. "I was crazy about boys at your age, and they were crazy about me, too. . . . I always used to have parties on Friday nights for all my friends, and after they left my mother and I would clean up together and talk everything over." However, Mimi has dreams of being in a fish's body, "gulping for air," or struggling to be released from her mother's suffocating involvement in her life. In Deborah Hautzig's young adult novel, *Second Star to the Right*, one of the most powerful instances of how Leslie is overwhelmed by her mother's covetous love occurs when she returns from a dance one evening. Her mother hands the phone to her so that Leslie can tell not only her mother, but her mother's friend about it:

> I spilled it all out, bubbles and all, with Mom sitting there, eating up every word. And the strangest feeling came over me as I talked—as though I were a float in Macy's Thanksgiving Day Parade and someone had poked a hole in me. The more I told Mom and Judy, the emptier I felt.[5]

This universal need to exclude one's parents from the contemplation of precious and private adolescent experiences occurs several times in Mazer's stories. In "Mimi the Fish" Mimi repeatedly tries to escape from her mother's questions about her date: "That fine swimming feeling, that lightness was draining away. Why couldn't her mother leave her alone?" Mazer's characters change and grow out of their past relationship with their parents, but they are aware that it's happening. Mimi's mother cries, and Mimi lets her mother hold her: "She bent her head, almost willingly. It was like a gift to her mother. . . . Because even now . . . she was moving away." And when Mama strokes Zoe's hair in "Peter in the Park," Zoe feels "faintly irritable"; she thinks to herself that her family doesn't know her like an open book, as they bragged: "You haven't read every one of my pages. Damn it, no!"

Chrissy of "Chocolate Pudding" lives in a trailer, functioning without friends or a reliable parent (her mother is dead and her father goes on extended drinking binges). By all rights Chrissy should be a miserable individual, but she copes well with her loneliness and is elated over her first romantic encounter. Like Chrissy, Louise, the heroine of "Guess Whose Friendly Hands," must accept a difficult situation. Louise, a cancer patient who knows she is dying, can accept the truth herself, but desperately needs an end to her mother's pretense that she will get better.

The portrayal of the protagonist of the unusual "Zelzah: A Tale

from Long Ago" does not stop with the adolescent years as in the
other stories, but goes on to show Zelzah in her forties. Sent to
the U.S. for a never-realized arranged marriage, Zelzah works
hard to live and to help others and becomes a self-supporting,
educated single woman who doesn't appear to lack for anything.
The independence she earns is a common theme in *Dear Bill,
Remember Me?*

Summer Girls, Love Boys, read as a whole, does not leave a
single dominant impression, as does Mazer's first collection. Mazer continues to write about girls who stand up for themselves,
girls who make a psychological break with their parents, and
girls who reject the domination of their boyfriends. While not
emphasized enough throughout the book to bind the collection
together, one theme that recurs to some extent is that of personal
courage, or the courage to be independent. "Amelia Earhart, Where
Are You When I Need You?" is an example of a successful treatment of this theme in *Summer Girls, Love Boys*. Desiring personal
courage, Phoebe regrets that she failed to hide from her eccentric
Aunt Clare her fear that her aunt might harm her. Less successful
because the concerns of its elderly protagonists are not the concerns of Mazer's teenage readers, "Down Here on Greene Street"
portrays a woman who must make the difficult choice between
staying alone where she has lived independently for seventy years,
or moving to Florida to live with her sweetheart. The collection
is framed by two poems that do not measure up to the literary
quality of the stories and suffers from the inclusion of the less
competent stories; moreover, the quality of the stories is more
uneven than in the first collection.

Edith Wharton wrote, "One of the fiction-writer's essential gifts
is that of discerning whether the subject which presents itself to
him, asking for incarnation, is suited to the proportions of a short
story or of a novel."[6] With one exception, Norma Fox Mazer chooses
her forms wisely.

Mazer's "Something Expensive" fails to work as a short story
because of its scope. As it opens, Mazer warns the reader that
things are not all well. Marylee's mother gives her a gift, and it
unsettles Marylee. The story's sense of foreboding grows, until

Marylee discovers that her mother is having an affair. The story's weakness is that Marylee bounces back from this devastating knowledge too quickly. At story's end, after only five pages, she is pleased with herself over an incident in which she overcomes her own "doormat" image and surmises that while she can't make her mother stop seeing a man, she can control her own life. Her too-quick recovery and acceptance of the situation, forced by the shortness of the form, is unrealistic and suggests that a novel might have been a better form for all the author has taken on in the story.

There are several similarities between one of Mazer's stories and one of her novels that enable us to see how she chooses the appropriate literary form for each. Chrissy in "Chocolate Pudding" recalls Joyce, of *Mrs. Fish, Ape, and Me, the Dump Queen.* In "Chocolate Pudding" Chrissy lives in a trailer with her uncle and her father. Alone much of the time and adjusted to her lonely life, she finds joy in a friendship with a boy from school. In *Mrs. Fish* Joyce is similarly isolated in her house by the county dump where she lives with Old Dad, her uncle. She has a hard time with other children at school, but she accepts her situation and adapts to their cruelty. In the novel she, too, finds a friend, though this time it's an adult, not another child. Mazer chooses the short story form for "Chocolate Pudding" because she wants to focus on one incident: the first time Chrissy invites the boy to visit her. But Mazer chooses to treat *Mrs. Fish* in novel form because the scope of the story is much broader, including more characters, more plot, and more challenges for her protagonist to face.

In "Chocolate Pudding" the story describes the family situation quickly, providing just enough background information about Chrissy's father and uncle to let readers understand her isolation. For example, one paragraph serves to describe the trailer's layout (and thereby Chrissy's living conditions), including a homey comment ("No more, no less than we need") that suggests Chrissy's ease and familiarity with describing it—and accepting it. The last sentence emphasizes her isolation, describing her sitting on her bed, looking out of the window, alone. The school setting enhances this image of a lonely girl who is on the outside of groups

of other girls: One of them might ask her for a cigarette, we are
told, but they show no further interest. The story then zeroes in
on the incident in which Chrissy finally finds a friend, a boy her
age who is persistent enough to make her acquaintance. Chrissy
worries during the school bus ride that her uncle and dad might
be drunk when they arrive at the trailer. Mazer takes little time
to develop the few characters in the story and concentrates on
the boy's visit. She uses the first person to set the tone as well
as to smoothly provide information about the setting and characters: Chrissy thinks matter-of-factly of how frail the trailer is,
imagining its flimsy, unsound condition. Though housing should
not be a child's concern, her thoughts underscore the weight of
the worries she must concern herself with.

In *Mrs. Fish,* on the other hand, Mazer introduces characters
and setting in a leisurely fashion, including the reproduction of
the dump sign, and adding epic-style lists of objects in the dump:

> There were pots with holes in them, pans without handles,
> glasses, jars, dishes, clothes, shoes and boots, curtains, radios
> by the dozen, lamps, tables, trunks, cribs, pictures and paint-
> ings, vacuum cleaners, sewing machines, plants, thermoses,
> skis and sleds, jars of pills and bottles of medicine, eyeglasses,
> and oh . . . everything. I never understood it. People spent all
> that money, and then they threw their things away.

Instead of describing scenes with a major character succinctly, as
in the story, Mazer here gives chapter-length treatment to scenes
with Mrs. Fish, complete with lengthy dialogue that explores the
woman's character. When Joyce visits Mrs. Fish in her office at
the school, we learn about the woman's family and her past as
she asks Joyce about herself.

The short story requires a subject or scope that is best treated
within the limits of the shorter form. The subject matter of Mazer's
stories can be broken down into two categories: the everyday
occurrences of home, family, and school as experienced by an
adolescent girl; and unusual topics such as terminal illness, factory worker organization, and an incident in the life of a mildly

retarded girl. In the former category is a typical story, "Avie Loves Ric Forever," which chronicles the friendship between two teenagers that develops into a romance. Examples of the second category are "Amelia Earhart, Where Are You When I Need You?", in which Phoebe's only alternative in a family emergency is to stay with Aunt Clare, who talks to herself and seems frightening; and "Carmella, Adelina, and Florry," in which a young woman is fired from her job after being a conspicuous part of a stop-work action in a factory.

Although her short stories usually occur over a brief time span, in an ordinary setting, Mazer can succeed with a time span over years, a setting over continents. In the aforementioned "Zelzah: A Tale from Long Ago" she writes convincingly of a Polish girl who comes to America alone, in steerage, and lives and works independently, educating herself and becoming a teacher. Consistently condensing the events of the long time span, Mazer does not lose touch with the small but crucial moments that stand out in Zelzah's life, like a moment when, as a girl, Zelzah stands surveying the farm where she works and thinks to herself that life is wonderful. The deft balancing of long periods of elapsed time with particular important moments make the story work.

The opposite of "Zelzah" in span of setting and plot is "Guess Whose Friendly Hands," which takes place during one day and is confined to the sickroom of Louise, a terminal cancer patient. With economy of action and setting, it is a powerful story, and Louise's moment of "extraordinary clarity," when she sees the beauty of her everyday setting and "how good everything was," at story's end is a triumph, though we know she will die. "Do You Really Think It's Fair?" is interesting, too, because the story takes place in the psychologist's office, and the device of having only the girl speak emphasizes this limited setting even more, and intensifies the effect upon the reader.

The protagonists of Mazer's short stories are almost always seen not only within the context of their school or social lives, but also in the context of their family lives. The attention Mazer pays to the family situation enhances the realism of her stories. The interactions between family members are more skillfully used in

the stories than they are in the novels, to create conflict quickly
or to define a character. The focus of the story remains on the
teenage protagonist, rather than shifting to the adult being in-
troduced. In this way the appearance of adult characters is well
integrated into the short fiction. The inclusion of family scenes
is a distinct aspect of Mazer's work that is better accomplished
in her stories than in her novels.

The family relationships in "Up on Fong Mountain" reveal the
main character: "My father says I'm stubborn as a bulldog," protagonist Jessie begins, relating a story of fighting over the newspaper that serves to draw Jessie's character. "Mom thinks she
and I are alike," she states, *"But* Mom doesn't say boo to Dad,
she's always very sweet to him. . . . I'm not like her in that way
at all. I'm not sweet." This shorthand characterization of her father and mother provides as much information about Jessie as it
does about her parents. Fourteen-year-old Zoe, in "Peter in the
Park," badly needs independence from her mother, her aunt, and
her grandmother, with whom she lives. When her need is referred
to teasingly as "rebellion in the ranks" by her aunt, Zoe's need
is more urgently felt. In "Summer Girls, Love Boys" Mary, her
parents' long-awaited, beloved only child, can no longer play a
childlike role in the family. Her mother is shocked by even the
suggestion that Mary have her long hair cut, and in the end Mary
resolutely cuts off her hair herself, a gesture of becoming less
sheltered, more open to the world outside her claustrophobic family that wins the reader's sympathy. The limits of the short story
form prevent Mazer from attempting to build sympathy for the
adults as she does in her novels, sometimes telling chapters from
an adult's point of view.

The form of a short story demands a quick development. The
author can't take an entire chapter to introduce a character or
spend much time in laying out the scene and creating the conflict.
Mazer is highly successful at the brief character sketch, the few
paragraphs that make the situation clear. The quick definition
of characters that she does so adeptly is demonstrated in "Mimi
the Fish":

In the shop . . . Mimi's mother was cheerful. . . . But in the apartment, in the rooms behind the butcher shop, Mimi's mother seemed to fade. She scrubbed the two spots of color off her cheeks and wore a faded housecoat that reached just below her knees.

Her father is described succinctly: He had

heavy white hairless arms and big heavy hands, raw-looking, like fresh meat. He rarely spoke. If an argument between Mimi and her mother or Mimi and her brother went on too long, if the voices rose beyond a certain threshold known only to him, he would bang on the door between the shop and the house, or heave himself up from his plush chair and boot Mimi in the rear end.

Mazer rises to the challenge of establishing character briefly in the short story form; she has created extremely vivid characters. A few, like Carol in "Why Was Elena Crying?", are not particularly memorable; Carol is not well drawn or very interesting. She envies her beautiful, even-tempered, smarter, nicer older sister; for Carol, everything seems to go wrong at school and at home, and to make things worse, she cries at the slightest provocation. Carol's story draws too neat a conclusion; she realizes that her sister's perfection "had been as much a burden to her as my crying had been to me."

Yet most of Mazer's characters are wonderfully realized, like Marlene in "How I Run Away and Make My Mother Toe the Line." Marlene is nothing like Mazer's well-spoken characters; she is "big and dumb"; she knows it, and she accepts it. She's twelve, and her best friend Lucy is eight. Her mother is not sensible enough to let Marlene study with Lucy in peace, and benefit from her help; but Marlene, despite her backwardness, seems wiser than her mother. She knows it was out of line for her mother to physically shove Lucy after she and Marlene made a mess in the apartment, and she has the sense to resist a boy's unwelcome advances, even using force to do so. Her story is told in her own voice, which enhances the effect of this excellent story.

In "Chocolate Pudding" lonely, wary Chrissy is convincingly won over and is visited by her first romantic friend. Mazer creates her home life and her isolation so beautifully that we admire the girl's strength and rejoice in her happiness when the gift of a friend makes her problems seem less important. Jessie in "Up on Fong Mountain" seems an archetype of a Mazer short story character: She is honest about her own faults, but she feels good about herself; she is an independent thinker, has a sense of humor, and can cope with people and situations while remaining true to herself.

Two characters who share an unusual trait are Bibi, from "De Angel and De Bow Wow," and Zelzah, from "Zelzah: A Tale from Long Ago." When the handsome Jimmy's mother dies, unattractive Bibi feels sorry for the helpless young man and sees her role in helping him out. She remembers her gift for raising her friend out of the doldrums, and she begins to help him; the two eventually marry. Equally selfless, Zelzah is defined by her service to others; her name means "Shade-in-the-Heat," and she is told, "You are meant to be a comfort to those around you." The two also share a practicality about romance: Bibi begins visiting Jimmy partly for romantic reasons, but also to help him, and she matter-of-factly thinks that they might be a good couple; Zelzah dutifully offers to marry the American she is supposed to wed through an arranged marriage, but when it does not come about, she has an impulse to laugh, and, as mentioned earlier, she thrives as a single woman.

One of the richest aspects of Mazer's short stories is her varied, unusual use of different points of view. They bring variety to the collections when they are read as a whole, and display her great skill in telling a story.

Third-person narrative can be found in stories like "De Angel and De Bow Wow," "Zelzah," and "Summer Girls, Love Boys"; the most poetic use of the form is in "Guess Whose Friendly Hands." In this story Louise, the eighteen-year-old girl who is dying from cancer while her mother and sister care for her at home, is shown longing for her relatives to acknowledge the truth. The omniscient narrative reveals her thoughts:

> No lies. . . . Till now, when the lies and half-truths, the evasions and secrets spun through the apartment like spider's filament, toughly frail, almost invisible, swaying in the slightest breeze. Louise longed to gather it all up, crush the frail webs in her hand, yet the thought of it made her heart beat up sickeningly into her throat.

The epistolary style used in "Dear Bill, Remember Me?" represents the consummate use of that form. In a series of letters begun and discarded, Mazer cleverly reveals to the reader a story of unrequited love. Only the last letter shown is actually sent, one that gives no hint of Kathy's true feelings.

An unsuccessful epistolary story, "Avie Loves Ric Forever," also relates the story of a romance in letters; but it lacks the impact of "Dear Bill" because it manipulates the epistolary form to let readers know the outcome of the tale. Richie doesn't send the letters she writes to her friend Stevie telling him that she's in love with him. Instead, she finally tells him in person, and happily learns that he returns her interest. However, to allow readers to know the outcome, Richie then finishes a letter explaining how she confessed her love to Stevie in person. It is implausible that she would write this last letter to Stevie, telling him of an event at which he was present—the letter is clearly intended only to fill in the reader. This obvious contrivance ruins the effectiveness of the story.

"Up on Fong Mountain" is told in journal entries, a very effective method that shows the character's worries, concerns, and personal feelings about herself and about trivial matters. She muses about being kissed, frets about her weight, and recounts a disturbing fight with her boyfriend. Elsewhere, Mazer is able to develop a vivid character without this first-person account of private thoughts, but it serves here to make Jessie a distinct character.

In "Carmella, Adelina, and Florry" Mazer uses her most unusual literary device: an oral history transcription. As an American History assignment, a student turns in the transcript of a tape she has made of her mother's recollections of working in a factory:

> I sat down on the iron stool, turned on the power, and watched the belt slipping around the arm. I was terrified as I slid the first piece of yellow mica under the arm and pressed the lever foot. *WHANG!* I had good reason to be scared. You could lose your fingers, with no trouble at all, to that arm.

This story could easily have been told in a straightforward first-person narrative, but the device chosen links Zelda and her daughter. Although almost the entire story consists of the transcript, the daughter's introduction reveals that the transcript has opened a whole new side of her mother to her. Since the mother is recalling her young adulthood, her story is of particular interest to young adult readers.

"How I Run Away . . ." is an ambitious example of first-person narrative. The form allows Mazer to create a fully developed character in the first four paragraphs of the story. With the storytelling logic of an unsophisticated child, Marlene begins, in her ungrammatical speech, by giving her name and relating how she signs it: Marlene M. T. Thornton. Mazer displays the girl's directness: "Nobody better not say nothing about my name. 'Cause if they do, I sure will beat their butt." Marlene is an endearing character, an unforgettable girl who comes alive through Mazer's extraordinary skill in presenting Marlene's thoughts and emotions through the consistent use of her narrative voice.

With a very different use of first-person narrative, in "Do You Really Think It's Fair?", Mazer starts her story abruptly and powerfully as Sara Gorelick reports to the school psychologist.

> Well, here I am.
> What? I'm Sara Gorelick! Didn't you ask me to come to your office? Mrs. Teassle *said*—Oh. No, I guess we haven't met before. But I know who *you* are. So, what's up?

. . . .

No, I don't want to be a movie star! A model? *No.*

Well . . . a judge.

Uh-huh. You heard me right. A judge. I don't think that's so funny. What's the hilarious joke? Yes, you are too laughing at me! I know when somebody is laughing and—Look, *you* asked me to come down here.

The entire story is Sara's half of her conversations with the psychologist. Through a series of meetings readers learn the setting, the personalities of both Sara and the psychologist, and the source of Sara's torment: Her sister was killed by a drunken driver. Sara's tough talk is believable, and the form of the narrative is fresh and exciting. The short story form is perfect for this unique narrative technique, which reveals so much with so few words. By answering questions, Sara relates the story of her sister's death; Mazer adds plot information by occasionally having the girl repeat the psychologist's comments. This device enhances the girl's jeering, mocking tone and does not detract from the flawless narrative.

Mazer's recent short story, "I, Hungry Hannah Cassandra Glen . . .," from *Sixteen,* is devastating in its revelation of the desperate situation of two teenage friends, Hannah and "Crow," whose families can't feed them properly. At the story's opening, upon the death of a shopkeeper they've both known, the narrator makes a shocking statement:

When Mr. Augustus Francher's heart burst, I told Crow we were going to the service at Bascind's Funeral Home because, afterward, at Mrs. Francher's house, there would be food.

"I, Hungry Hannah" is an example of the way Mazer has perfected her short story style, revealing, at a rapid pace, the terrible position the two teenagers are in, adding subtle details such as having a character write with a pencil rather than using up the ink in a ball-point pen in order to demonstrate her poverty. The narrator's ruthlessly matter-of-fact statement at the story's beginning makes her unexpected reaction to seeing the body more poignant: "My eyes filled. Just then I understood that he was dead and what it meant."

The high degree of sophistication in the style of "How I Run Away and Make My Mother Toe the Line," "Do You Really Think It's Fair?," and "I, Hungry Hannah Cassandra Glen . . ." exemplifies Mazer's mastery of the short story form. If, as Poe writes, "the unity of effect or impression is a point of the greatest importance,"[7] then Norma Fox Mazer must be considered a resounding success in her use of the form.

4. The Message

Along with the sheer pleasure of reading that Norma Fox Mazer's books and stories provide, one of the most important aspects of her work is the message that she gives to her readers. This message is inspirational, but not didactic; it is a thought-provoking view presented through the lives of her characters. Mazer presents certain themes over and over again, basic ideas that intrigue her, that appeal to her intellect.

Similarly, Mazer often writes about characters who are reminiscent of characters in previous books and stories. Unconsciously or not, she will present a scene in a book or story that she has delineated before and show different characters reacting to the same situation. Though she is an experimenter, a writer who does not hesitate to produce a book that is stylistically unlike anything she's done before, her characters are often familiar, turning over in their minds the problems and hopes and choices experienced by a previous Mazer character. Character and theme are inseparable in her works: If we run across a very independent young woman in two of her works, a theme in both works is liable to be independence. For this reason, a discussion of her characters is intrinsic to a discussion of her themes.

Mazer is interested in ethical dilemmas, such as the justification and consequences of a parent kidnapping his own child, or the problems and consequences of a politically active couple giving up their child and going underground when they are sought by the police. Mazer is also interested in ideas such as the existence

of a matriarchal society, and the importance of the female in such
a culture as compared with our own; yet the ideas and the dilemmas she explores are presented in the framework of stories about
contemporary teenage protagonists who move in the settings and
in the plots she devises, reacting in ways that instill hope in those
who read about how characters overcome adversity, behave independently, cope with being an outsider, and react to hypocrisy.
Mazer takes her characters'—and her readers'—problems seriously. She places her characters in situations that demand a great
deal from them, and she does not let her characters down; they
respond powerfully, underlining her themes.

The themes that Mazer explores are vital to her teenage readers. Strong themes are crucial to any affecting works of fiction,
and Mazer's recurring themes, one of which may dominate one
novel and put in a cameo appearance as a subtheme in another,
are clear and important to her audience.

The most admirable message that Mazer delivers to her readers
is: Although life isn't easy, "don't despair. There is strength inside
you."[1] Her professed ambition of instilling hope is realized in, for
example, *Taking Terri Mueller,* in which her character draws
upon her emotional strength and overcomes a difficult situation.
Terri has been comfortable for years with her loving father, who,
however, kidnapped her from her mother after he lost custody of
the small child. Against his wishes and in the face of his sarcasm
and discouragement, Terri insists on seeking out her mother.

> "I called California today," Terri said. . . . "Oakland. I got
> the number of K. Mueller from the operator, and I called after
> school." It was too bad the way her heart was pulsing. "I thought
> K. Mueller might be my mother."
> He put down the spoon. "Was it?"
> "No." Her braid swung over one shoulder. "I tried Kathryn
> Susso, too, and Kathryn Bradshaw."
> "Busy, weren't you?" he said.
> Sarcasm? She wasn't used to that from him. But then, this
> was a whole new world.

This courage is embodied by most of Mazer's protagonists. The
problem facing Terri Mueller is an exceptionally difficult one, but

almost all of Mazer's characters face problems and difficult situations, whether they are unusual or whether they are common dilemmas of teenagers.

In *I, Trissy* Trissy must face a difficult and enormously upsetting situation, that of her parents separating. Her spirited, indignant reactions, if not socially correct, seem reasonable, given her character. Readers who vicariously enjoy Trissy's sometimes outrageous behavior are witnessing a human being reacting to and adjusting to her situation and one who is eventually strong enough to accept that her parents will not get together again.

Jenny, in *A Figure of Speech*, cannot solve all the problems she faces with her grandfather's ailing health; her parents hold all the power in the decision of what happens to Grandpa. The family plan of putting Grandpa into a nursing home is unacceptable to her, and she unhesitatingly follows when he leaves home. This is an impractical solution to Jenny's problem, but readers are shown Jenny's sense of injustice and her resolve in the face of her family's plans for Grandpa.

A veritable tower of strength is Finn in *Up in Seth's Room*. This forceful character demonstrates the theme of finding strength inside yourself. In the novel, everyone wants something from Finn, including her parents, who want her to drop Seth. Finn does one of the most difficult and courageous things any of Mazer's characters do: She tells her parents she is going to disobey them and she continues to see Seth. Finn tells them she wants to be treated "like a real person," allowed to choose her own boyfriend. It is not easy, and she has to force herself to keep her eyes on her father's face. "Please, Dad . . . I'm growing up . . . I don't do it to make you feel bad. You and Mom raised me right. Don't you believe that? You don't have to worry about me."

Although she is disobeying her parents, Finn struggles to keep their love. She begs them to stop fighting with her. "Don't be mad at me anymore. I'm your daughter." She hugs her father, crying, "Remember me? I'm Finn." He is responsive, but "right then she felt something happening, something changing. She felt it like a wind rushing past her, brushing her skin." What Finn feels is the exhilaration of having stood up for herself.

Finn has won, but she lets her parents win, too, by setting the hour when she must return from seeing Seth. Finn overcomes both peer pressure and her parents' narrow-mindedness. She confronts everyone, she makes a compromise with her parents, the only ones who really have a say in what she does, and she continues to see Seth. Readers are shown that none of this pressure need push them to do things they don't want to, that they may argue with their parents' ultimatums.

Joyce, the young protagonist of *Mrs. Fish, Ape, and Me, the Dump Queen*, must also test the limits of her courage and determination. She survives the terrifying stroke suffered by her guardian, Old Dad, going against his wishes to call upon another adult for help. She then deals with the old man's exasperating stubbornness, which almost has the tragic result of sending her friend Mrs. Fish out of their lives. Readers witness Joyce's strength and recognize the limits of her abilities to cope with problems. There is an appropriate time for Joyce to ask a sympathetic adult for help, unlike the situation in *A Figure of Speech*, where Jenny does not have any such adult sympathetic to her and Grandpa's problems to whom she could turn.

Jenny Pennoyer, reappearing in *When We First Met*, recalls Finn in that she decides to continue to see her parentally forbidden, "star-crossed" boyfriend. As Finn did, Jenny makes a difficult attempt to legitimize her romance by confronting her parents about the boyfriend. In this case, she shocks the family by introducing them to Rob—who is the son of the drunk driver who killed Jenny's sister—without preparing them for the news by telling them whom she is dating. Readers can see the folly of this act, and its consequences are realistic. Jenny is a girl who is at odds with her whole family, more so than Finn in *Up in Seth's Room*. It is not surprising that she handles the meeting so badly. It is more intriguing to witness Finn handling her family. She demands their respect, as when she elicits a response from her sister Maggie that makes her feel "like another person," not like a younger sister.

In *Someone to Love* the most important unpleasant situations that Nina copes with are parting with Mitch and having sex with one of her professors, once, in a weak moment. Nina's greatest triumphs are not over situations, however, but attitudes. Mazer shows readers the cynical attitudes toward love of both Mitch and Nancy, Nina's sister. Mitch thinks that "Nobody knows anybody," so he doesn't believe in a true love, as Nina does. Nancy is the party girl who doesn't want to settle down with one person. The author lets readers know that these other views exist; she also shows them that Nina knows they exist, and that Nina, finding strength inside herself, remains firm in her belief that there is such a thing as real, lasting love, and that she hopes to find it.

The emotional strength that Mazer's female characters learn to rely on is missing from many of her male characters. Rather than exemplifying Mazer's message themselves, her males serve as challenges that the females must stand up to. Mitch, in *Someone to Love*, tries Nina when he states, "A man's feelings aren't like a woman's." Seth, in *Up in Seth's Room*, speaks of "the male creed. . . . It means that the macho thing to do with a girl is never take no for an answer. Just keep trying. Wear her down. . . ." In *Three Sisters* most of the men are unpleasant characters. While the father is a weak, shadowy figure, Karen's boyfriend David drops her when she insists on keeping her virginity; Tobi's boyfriend Jason is a brutal drunk; and Liz's boyfriend Scott is untrue to her. Men and boys, thus, often make Mazer's protagonists confront life's difficulties.

Certainly Karen, in *Three Sisters*, suffers from life's slings and arrows; she feels unspecial, she misses the closeness she used to feel with her two sisters, and her boyfriend breaks up with her. A common difficulty that many adolescents face is the anguish of having done things that they later regret. Karen makes a play for her sister's fiancé, and unfortunately, he plays along for a while. Karen's chagrin after he has stopped playing is severe, but Mazer once again instills hope in readers, the hope that they can overcome situations that seem unbearable, even if they have created their own difficulties.

The strength of Mazer's characters is often tested by their inability to change bad circumstances. Jenny in *A Figure of Speech* is a prime example of a girl with such a disturbing problem. She is powerless to keep her grandfather from being forced to give up his basement apartment, and she is powerless to keep him from being placed in a nursing home. She acts irresponsibly, to go with him when he takes the initiative to avoid the nursing home. She is a child in a family where the adults decide what is to be done, even if all the adults (including Jenny's brother and his bride) act unfairly. Unable to accept the situation, Jenny acts unwisely.

Trissy in *I, Trissy* is another girl frustrated by a problem she can't solve, but she finally learns to accept her situation. The novel charts her rejection and eventual acceptance of her parents' separation. Mazer's other middle-grade-school protagonist, Joyce, in *Mrs. Fish . . .*, is able to effect some changes in her life, but not others, and she is able to realize what she can change and what she must accept. Although anxious about the crisis of Old Dad's stroke, she seeks help from Mrs. Fish. Yet when she is treated as an outcast by the other children in school, she knows she can't do anything to change the situation; she must accept it, and summon her dignity to withstand the endless mistreatment she receives. She is so accustomed to her way of handling abuse from other children that when Mrs. Fish is ridiculed at school, and doesn't react as Joyce would, Joyce is angry with Mrs. Fish, not with the children who are making fun of Mrs. Fish:

> I hated Mrs. Fish. I didn't even know her, and I hated her! She was making a fool of herself. My fists clenched. "Stop it," I said. "Stop it. Stop it!"

Some protagonists must summon their inner resolve in order to make their own difficult decisions. As discussed above, Finn in *Up in Seth's Room* makes the crucial decision to see Seth against her parents' wishes, and Jenny chooses to see Rob in similar circumstances in *When We First Met*. As Rhoda says to Jenny in that novel, "You can't make decisions about your life based on what's going to make everyone else happy." Mazer's characters show her readers that some circumstances cannot be changed, and she shows how strong girls adapt to these circumstances. She also shows them that, with courage, there is hope for change in difficult situations and that girls like Mazer's readers can make decisions and changes to make things better.

Independence is a major theme that runs through Mazer's writing. Her characters are often seen breaking away from parents or guardians, outgrowing childhood. They make things happen, rather than letting things happen to them. In this way, they are making their own choices. They also take responsibility for their actions and become more responsible by starting to get along without the protection they've begun to resent having.

An interesting picture of independence is the ultimate situation of Zelzah in the story, "Zelzah: A Tale from Long Ago." Zelzah is an immigrant who comes to the United States for an arranged marriage. After giving up her family and crossing the ocean, she is jilted for another girl. She does not marry, but studies at night, after working in a factory all day, to become a schoolteacher. She cares for her students. She turns down offers to meet eligible men, and rents an apartment with "her own entrance" and "a tiny but efficient kitchen," and visits her sister and her family every summer. She made one request to her fiancé; she had never asked anyone for anything before. The wish was, "I would like a cat when we have our own home." And when she lives by herself in the apartment, she has her cats. Mazer writes, "Was she happy? Who could say?" but the picture she paints of Zelzah's independent life seems to be just what Zelzah wishes.

Independence in Mazer's fiction sometimes means independence from the unwelcome influence of men upon her characters. Zelzah's example is a bit severe; her arranged marriage did not work out, and she rejects several opportunities to meet or become friendly with other men. Fifteen-year-old Jessie Granatstein in "Up on Fong Mountain" is a prime example of Mazer's showing her readers how an independent protagonist rejects the domination of a boyfriend. Jessie and her boyfriend BD disagree about what to do one evening, and when BD accuses her of being "picky," she gives in, only to think later, "I realized, just like that, he had talked me out of what I wanted to do and into what he wanted to do." Their disagreements mount until they have a serious fight about what to do one night, when BD wants to go to a movie. "I haven't made up my mind what I want to do tonight," Jessie tells him. "Nobody asked me what I wanted to do, only told me what they wanted to do." They break off the romance after another exchange in which Jessie complains,

> "We're going to do this, we're going to do that, we're going here, we're eating this—don't you think I have a mind of my own? You want your own way all the time. You never ask me anything. You just barrel on ahead. You want to lead me around by the nose!"

No reader can be in doubt about Jessie's sense of independence after this speech, and Mazer shows that girls can be independent.

A strong theme of independence also runs through the story "Mimi the Fish," which begins with a girl dreaming of being a fish, swimming from murky water up into the light. Mimi's mother wants to relive her own past through Mimi and she asks the details of Mimi's first date. The mother eventually breaks down and cries about Mimi's growing up, and though Mimi is kind to her, mentally she is detached as she allows her mother to hold her; she is "moving away . . . out of this life, these closed rooms, swimming free, swimming toward her own life." Mazer knows that adolescents must have this autonomy, that they must break away from their parents and from childhood. Many of the stories have themes of breaking away from parents or other caretaking adults. In "Peter in the Park" Zoe is severely protected by three loving but smothering women. Her first foray into rebelliousness results in a friendship with a strange man. Going into the park is forbidden to Zoe; talking with the man must be far worse. The girl imagines her grandmother's reaction: "If Marcia knew, oh wow, she'd go up in smoke for sure." Zoe is another Mazer character who is seen wanting her thoughts and secrets to remain her own.

In "Summer Girls, Love Boys" Mary is as sheltered as Zoe in "Peter in the Park." She is the only child of two loving parents, and feels terribly sorry for them because she knows she is growing apart from them. Still, she cuts off her hair, a gesture that symbolizes cutting ties with them. In both stories Mazer shows that protagonists can be loving, yet still need desperately to break away. Rhoda, Jenny's friend in *When We First Met,* is similar to Zoe and Mary. She is too pampered, she must make her own way, and she decides not to attend college as expected, but to get a job and an apartment after high school, and to live on her own. Again Mazer makes it clear that independence is crucial to her characters.

Fights with parents are dramatic examples of the difficult but necessary process of breaking away in order to grow up. Finn's mother, in *Up in Seth's Room,* seems utterly without understanding as she forbids Finn to see Seth. Jenny Pennoyer and her mother get along like oil and water, and this is not an unusual relationship between mother and daughter in Mazer's fiction. The fights underline the distance between parent and child as a child grows into an adolescent.

Relationships among women and girls are a crucial aspect of Mazer's work. From the slap Trissy receives from her mother after she finds Trissy's "Memo to My Mother," there is a train of incidents of mother-daughter antagonism. Jenny is slapped, in *A Figure of Speech,* and feels, like Trissy, that she's not liked as much as the other children in her family are. I have already recounted the tense conversation between mother and daughter in *Up in Seth's Room;* at one point, Finn turns on her mother: "It was always easier to be mad at her mother than at her father." The strained relationship is obvious in the following exchange, when Finn is standing before a mirror, feeling her swollen glands and sticking out her tongue.

Her mother stopped at her door.

"Aren't you going to school?"
Finn blew her nose. "I'm sick."
"You look okay to me."
"Some nurse."
"Does anything hurt?" her mother said crisply.
"Everything." She fell back on the bed and pulled the blanket over her head.

Three Sisters is a book that examines not only the sisters' relationships but also the mother-daughter one. In one scene the daughter is the one who invades the mother's privacy, by reading a book review she has written.

Not all relationships between protagonists and a mother, or aunts, or other older women are antagonistic. Though Zoe in "Peter in the Park" needs to break free from her family, the women who live with her are loving, caring, and special to her. The most congenial women characters appear in *Saturday, the Twelfth of October,* the fantasy that features a matriarchal society. In this idealized, peaceful society Mazer's characters get along well, but when Mazer writes contemporary realism, they fight with each other.

As Mazer explores aspects of independence throughout her fiction, she often writes about a protagonist working or hunting for a job. Holding a job is seen as a mature and independent thing to do, and finding a job shows that the world outside of home and school is hard. Several of Mazer's characters, including Karen in *Three Sisters* and Seth in *Up in Seth's Room,* are demoralized after searching for a job, for example, and some who have found work are treated badly by their employers.

Mazer likes to show independent characters who make things happen, rather than let things happen to them, and she shows the difference between them. In "Peter in the Park," Zoe takes control of her own actions by taking her forbidden walk in the park. She opens up her own life to new experience and thinks: "Imagine: if she had never gone into the park she would never have met Peter. . . . Is all life so chancy?" At least Zoe has made her life less chancy by taking the initiative to take her walk in the park. When Karen in *Three Sisters* makes things happen, she does so in a more direct way: She charges into a situation with a plan and determination. She goes after her sister's boyfriend deliberately, demonstrating that Mazer characters don't always act with great judgment. Her independent-minded characters may make mistakes, but her readers see them making decisions and controlling what happens to them.

Taking responsibility for one's independent actions is an idea that Mazer writes about in many stories. In *Someone to Love* the professor who had sex with Nina incenses her when he tries to take responsibility for what happened. He tells her, "I wanted it to happen. . . . Did you know that?" She thinks, "Had it all happened, then, because *he* had made it happen? And where was she in that scene?" This reaction is similar to Karen's in *Three Sisters*. Karen thinks about the kiss between her and Scott, her sister's fiancé. Her grandmother has just said to her, "Don't hope for things, Karen. Make them happen. Just do it." Karen thinks, "The kiss—had she made that happen? Or had he? Or had it just happened?" Later in the novel Mazer emphasizes that control is positive and desirable. Scott comes to Karen, after their romantic encounters are in the past, and, miserably, apologizes for them and therefore claims them as his responsibility. "Do you know what I'm saying?" he asks Karen. "I'm taking responsibility, Karen, for that morning, for the things you did—." When Karen reacts, Mazer is underlining the importance of being culpable for one's own actions: "That shocked her into anger. Take responsibility for what she did? It was theft. 'Oh, no you don't,' she said, 'Oh, no you don't.'" Mazer demonstrates that the need to be independent is strong, and the state of being independent is one to be prized.

Another important message that Mazer communicates throughout her fiction is that it is difficult to be an outsider. Because of their inner strength, various outsiders are seen adapting to their situations. Joyce, of *Mrs. Fish, Ape, and Me, the Dump Queen,* is ostracized because her guardian, Old Dad, runs the town dump. A boy in school recites a ditty he has invented about her: *"Orange peel* in her ear . . . She—smells—queer!" Chrissy in "Chocolate Pudding" chats with girls at school, but even though friendships progress to the point where a girl might telephone Chrissy, she ultimately goes her own way again, as there is no phone in the run-down trailer she lives in, far from the neighborhoods where her classmates live. Jenny in *A Figure of Speech* knows how tough it is to be an outsider in her own family, the only one who sees things from her grandfather's point of view.

Mazer includes some minor characters in her fiction who are

outsiders, usually because they are overweight. There is an overweight girl in *Someone to Love,* who is commented upon, as there is in *Up in Seth's Room.* Jerry, the boy Finn doesn't like, states, "Look at Brenda . . . What a character. She ought to lose about fifty pounds." "Maybe she doesn't want to," Finn replies. Later in the book Finn's friend Vida makes a small comment about Brenda, who through Finn's eyes "looked impressive in a flaming red dress" and who has a good voice. Vida says, "I'd have a good voice, too, if I weighed two hundred pounds." Vida's boyfriend dislikes the comment.

Mrs. Fish, who is overweight, is described by Joyce, who loves her, as "big, fat, strong, and beautiful." In *Mrs. Fish* . . . this theme gets its most thoughtful treatment, as both Mrs. Fish and Old Dad are unusual looking; Old Dad is called Ape because of his unusual body. Mrs. Fish chides him for suggesting that she call him Ape, as others do. He asks why she shouldn't and she answers: "What we look like is only a little part of the story, it's only the outside of the package. The real you is like a light shining through."

Sometimes characters feel like outsiders because they long for a boyfriend they don't have, especially when it seems that everyone else has one. Wanting someone to love is a notion that Mazer explores in several books. In *Up in Seth's Room* Finn feels "hollow" and "empty" after being physically close to a boy she does not care about. She is lonely and imagines that she might die before loving someone: She thinks of "never being in love, never having someone of her own. . . . I want someone, too," she says. Her friend Vida echoes this sentiment when Vida breaks up with her steady boyfriend. She says, "It's a really lonesome feeling to wake up in the morning and think I have no one to see in school." When Jenny first sees Rob in *When We First Met,* she has the same yearning to be in love: "Something winged and strong beat inside her. Was this the unnameable 'it' for which she had been waiting so long?"

The strongest embodiment of this theme is the book with the message in its title: *Someone to Love.* Nina "was nineteen and had no one. Had never had someone special and close. There was a hunger in her, a hunger for a friend and a lover. For a loving friend." She sees a couple on the street, wearing look-alike sweaters: "There was something beyond clothes or words. An aura that was almost visible, a *coupleness* that drew Nina's eyes." Nina, eager to have her own love, finds her lover, Mitch, and they move in together, "Melding . . . their individuality," gaining the "usness" she wanted. Just before the confrontation that causes them to break up, she sees that the campus is "packed with couples." Though Nina's affair with Mitch was not the ultimate love, it seems that, with her vision of the sky "wide, and blue as a plate" at the novel's end, she will find her someone. Mazer has pinpointed a common desire of her readers and has explored one girl's experience in being part of a couple.

In addition to showing many characters coping with being outsiders, Mazer shows how her protagonists react against hypocrisy. The truth, Mazer shows, is preferable to euphemisms and lies. This major theme gets full treatment in several of her books. In *Taking Terri Mueller,* for example, Terri discovers that for almost all her life she has believed a lie that her father has told her: that her mother died when she was small. She must come to terms with this monstrous lie, which he has long since justified to himself. The lie is unacceptable to the woman Terri's father is becoming close to and she stops seeing him, but a girl cannot similarly dismiss her father; she must accept that the deceit has taken place and reform her relationship with her father.

Downtown is a novel that is essentially about secrets; Peter has his secret from the world, that his politically minded parents are fugitives and, unintentionally, murderers. His girlfriend, Cary, has a less dramatic secret: She keeps from people that she is a foster child, her mother is a dope addict, and her father an alcoholic bum. The need for secrecy is symbolized by the fact that even Pete's name is a false one. In *Downtown* readers see that the actions of Pete's and Cary's parents have forced them to live with deceit.

Mazer's crowning achievement in dealing with her major theme of hypocrisy, however, is *A Figure of Speech*. People "never said what they really meant," Jenny muses. The character sympathetic to Jenny, Grandpa, rejects the euphemisms offered by his son when he calls dying "passing away." Jenny thinks: "Pretty words for ugly things! Grandpa hated those cover-up words, those figures of speech, and now so did she!" Throughout the book Jenny's family manipulates Grandpa, making logical and reasonable-sounding excuses for actions such as making him give up his basement apartment to live upstairs, and later to move to a nursing home. Jenny's parents have ways of rationalizing their actions, but uncompromising Jenny won't accept the rationalizations. One night Jenny overhears her parents recount a version of how Grandpa died as they play cards with friends:

> Jenny put her head down on the table. . . . . she could still hear them, going on and on about Grandpa: ". . . he just lay down and died, as if he knew it was his time . . . didn't suffer a bit . . . a real comfort to us that he went so easily . . ." Who are they talking about, she wondered. Who? And then she had to get out of there. She had to run out of the house, run long enough to outrun the sad, hypocritical voices.

The same theme pervades "Guess Whose Friendly Hands," the story about the cancer patient being taken care of by her mother and sister. The dying girl can be at peace only when the truth about her fate prevails among the three.

Mazer's protagonists show an aversion to deceiving their parents. In *Up in Seth's Room* Finn awkwardly lies about who is on the phone; she says "Beth" when it is actually the forbidden Seth on the other end of the line. Similarly, Jenny in *When We First Met* tells her parents she's meeting "Robin," the name of her boyfriend, but, uncomfortably, she lets her parents think that "Robin" is a girl. In both books the protagonists end their deceptions and confront their parents with the truth. Finn tells her parents she will continue to see Seth, and they impose conditions. Jenny brings Rob home to meet her family and to resolve the problem that he is who he is. To their incredulity at her action, she replies, "Would you rather I sneaked around? Would you rather I gave him a false name?" Finn, in arguing her point with her parents, reacts similarly: "Why don't you just come right out and say what you really mean? . . . you're afraid I'll have sex with Seth."

Also in *Up in Seth's Room* Finn isn't exactly lied to, but truly betrayed by Seth. After telling her he wouldn't expect to have sex with her, Seth tries to press Finn, until she has to fight him and run away from him. She asks,

> ". . . In your room, that whole thing—why did you do that?"
>
> "I don't know," he said.
>
> "Yes! You know," she insisted. "I told you—didn't I tell you how I felt?"
>
> "Well, I thought you were just saying that." He dug his hands into his pockets.
>
> "No, I don't understand you. Why would I just say it?"
>
> "Girls do—"
>
> "No," she said. "No. Why do you say such a terrible thing? I never faked you out. Whatever I felt, I told you. We talked about it. You remember! Why didn't you believe me?"

An idea that is repeated in Mazer's books is the injustice and hypocrisy of having one set of rules for kids, another for adults. When Jenny's parents are rude to Grandpa in *A Figure of Speech,* she complains that they are not respecting their elders, as she's told to do. They tell her to be quiet, and she thinks, "One law for *them,* another for kids." Finn, in *Up in Seth's Room,* receives a postcard from her father and doesn't want to let her mother see it. "You never let me see the letters he writes you!" says Finn. When her mother explains, "That's different," Finn says, "It's always different when it's you. . . . One set of rules for you. Right? And another for me."

Just as themes recur in Mazer's books, so do characters and scenes that illustrate those themes. Mazer has even repeated characters used in previous books. *When We First Met* can be called a sequel to *A Figure of Speech,* in which Jenny Pennoyer first appears, but when Mazer chooses, in *Someone to Love,* to revive the character Mitch Beers, who played a bit part as the obnoxious brother in *I, Trissy,* she is really taking advantage of the fact that she already knows Mitch's family well, having created them in *I, Trissy*. Those who read *I, Trissy* at a younger age will be informed that Trissy now attends college.

Certain scenes are familiar from one book to another. In *Someone to Love* Nina, going alone to a party, gets tipsy. It's a humorous scene, and similar to one in *Up in Seth's Room,* when Finn drinks too much at a party she attends without Seth. When a couple fights with each other, the reader recalls other fights, like Seth and Finn fighting in *Up in Seth's Room* and Mitch and Nina fighting in *Someone to Love*.

Three scenes in three different books have the same atmosphere, when a character confronts his or her parents with a romantic situation. In *A Figure of Speech* Vince shocks everyone by bringing home his new wife; in *When We First Met* Jenny's forbidden boyfriend unsubtly appears and causes turmoil in the family; in *Up in Seth's Room* Finn's older sister Maggie brings home the boy she is living with, and they tensely have a cup of tea in the kitchen with Maggie's mother. *Three Sisters* has a similar scene: a meeting between Tobi's disapproved-of boyfriend and her family in which the characters have a meal together. As Mazer explores recurrent themes in her books and stories, she draws upon similar characters and relationships.

Mazer's messages make her books not just entertainments, but inspiring, thought-provoking works. Her ideas make readers see things in a new light, and she presents situations that readers can apply to their own lives. Besides being pleasurable to read, her books are informative, rare, and valuable in that they can instill hope in readers who may feel overwhelmed by their own circumstances. Mazer can be recommended to any readers who might need to find the "strength inside" of themselves.

5. Within and Without

Within: The Author and Her Characters

Realism in characterization and setting is the most important of the aspects that define a novel as young adult literature. Readers of young adult fiction must be able to identify with protagonists' problems, concerns, or situations. Norma Fox Mazer is a writer who portrays believable characters in the most realistic settings, and she makes a point of showing her characters doing everyday things.

Mazer's realism succeeds particularly well when she writes about working-class people. In *When We First Met* Jenny's father is a store manager. Her brother is a mailman, and had worked in a box factory. Zan's father in *Saturday, the Twelfth of October* drives a truck for a newspaper service. In *Up in Seth's Room* Finn's father almost doesn't get home in time to spend New Year's Eve with his family because he's a trucker, and in *Taking Terri Mueller* Phil, Terri's father, is a fix-it man. Some young men choose the working class as opposed to going to college. Seth has done farm work, construction, and dishwashing, and has been a truck driver and a short-order cook. Mitch, Nina's boyfriend in *Someone to Love,* paints houses, and Scott, Liz's fiancé in *Three Sisters,* is a carpenter.

Living conditions are carefully drawn in Mazer's novels to reflect working-class characterization. The Pennoyer household is crowded; so is Zan Ford's, as she sleeps on a cot in the kitchen.

In "Mimi the Fish" Mimi rejects the idea her mother poses of giving a party at home: "What kind of party could they have in the space behind the butcher shop that served as living room, dining room, and kitchen for Mimi's family? There was barely space enough for the four of them. . . ." Mimi lists the appliances and furniture that crowd their rooms. Some of Mazer's characters live in trailers and have no telephones. In "I, Hungry Hannah . . ." characters actually go hungry. Jenny works in a fast-food restaurant in *When We First Met,* and the kinds of things boys and girls do on dates are buy food in a grocery store, ride a bus, and go to a park.

Many characters are seen looking for work; Mazer holds working in great importance, as described in *Up in Seth's Room:*

> "It's a dog of a job," he said. "I hate it. I'm going to quit."
> "Oh." She felt foolish, young, innocent. She felt at a disadvantage. Not his equal. He knew about the world. He worked. He quit jobs, took other jobs. He had a weary look to his face. It silenced her.

Seth holds a job in a restaurant where his crabby boss interferes with their meeting there, the only place they can meet; a similar scene occurs in *Downtown.* Characters in *Someone to Love,* in *Up in Seth's Room,* and in *Three Sisters* feel depressed because they cannot find jobs. Their searches are familiar experiences for readers, and holding a job means maturity and independence to Mazer's characters. As in contemporary society, home situations are not always traditional nuclear families in young adult literature, and are hardly ever so in Mazer's books. There is fighting between parents in *Saturday, the Twelfth of October* and in "Something Expensive" as well as in *Three Sisters.* The protagonist of *Downtown* is taken care of by his uncle, as Joyce is in *Mrs. Fish, Ape, and Me, the Dump Queen.* In the latter book Joyce is stumped by a theme assignment in school that must begin "I wish my parents would . . ."; she has no parents. Seth's mother left home when he was in junior high school, he informs Finn. The books are full of characters who have had a hard life.

Some of the topics that are treated in the fiction—drunken driving, parental kidnapping—are common crimes in our society, and some of the characters are even criminals—Phil, an adult in *Taking Terri Mueller,* for example. Mazer is chronicling contemporary family life, mainly in the working class, and her characters are authentic. The daughter of working-class parents herself, she is able to draw on her own experiences and feelings to portray working-class girls realistically.

Dorothy Briley, an editor of books for children and young adults, believes that certain authors write most effectively about a certain age:

> They remember what life felt like when they were the age of
> their character, and they are able to transmit those feelings
> through their character's response to the things that happen
> in the story. . . . Nina Bawden, for instance, [has] . . . a spe-
> cial memory of how she felt about herself, her parents, friends,
> and others when she was twelve.[1]

There is a presence of "character-memory," as Briley calls this special memory of a certain age, in Mazer's work. The character she brings alive with the most immediacy can be described thus: She is an intelligent fifteen-year-old. She lives among women or other girls to whom she reacts in an antagonistic way (particularly to her mother). Quick to anger or to sense injustice, she often feels the flush of strong emotion on her face. She's independent-minded, but not so much of a feminist that boys are unimportant to her; on the contrary, she often defies her parents in order to pursue a forbidden romance, a boy who is usually older than she. Either she falls in love in a traditional, romantic way, such as spotting a boy across the room and hoping to bump into him at school, or she takes the bull by the horns and goes after her romantic interest, making things happen.

Mazer may be drawing upon her own experiences as a girl growing up in a working-class family, but is Norma Fox Mazer Trissy? Is she any of her protagonists? One does encounter in her fiction many parallels with her life. Occupations such as working

in a bakery, driving a truck, and being a carpenter appear in
Mazer's family history as well as in her fiction. Her small-town
settings seem to describe Glens Falls, New York, where she grew
up. At least once, she has used a family surname for a character,
and two of her older male characters, Grandpa in *A Figure of
Speech* and Old Dad in *Mrs. Fish, Ape, and Me, the Dump Queen*,
left school at a young age, as Mazer's grandfather did. Another
parallel between her life and her fiction is that she often writes
about girls who fall in love with older men, and she, at the age
of seventeen, fell in love with Harry Mazer when he was about
twenty-three.

Real life and fiction seem to meet, also, in that Mazer, one of
three sisters, had three daughters who, of course, also comprise
such a triumvirate. Her exploration of sisters, not to mention of
relationships among women and girls, culminates in her recent
novel, *Three Sisters*.

While Mazer does seem to tap some of her own experiences for
her fiction, her writing is not necessarily autobiographical. To
assume that would make light of the artist's powers of imagination, of her propensity to think "What if? . . .," to follow her
creative idea to its unique conclusion, and of her ability to create
a character out of whole cloth.

Does Mazer have a temper as her protagonists sometimes do?
She has said,

> When I wrote *Trissy*, I wrote something that's not at all like
> me. I never blew up. Lately I've had a little different feeling.
> Probably this person with a temper is a person inside me . . .
> that person that I didn't let out. It has to be part of me because
> I'm writing about it.

Having a temper as Trissy does could be "part of" Mazer; writers
of fiction can transform experience into art, but they can also
create art from what they imagine.

As for the origins of the vivid women—strong, loving, caring—
in books like *Dear Bill*, Mazer believes that the women are a
combination of someone she has known and someone she would

like to have known. The grandfather in *A Figure of Speech* is also probably an amalgam of characters she has observed and thought about; and, she says, "old men get me right in the heart." She is at a loss to explain this fondness because she never knew her own grandfathers.

Although many aspects of Mazer's background and of her family appear in her fiction, it would be a dubious conclusion indeed to assume that she writes primarily autobiographical fiction. Rather than merely relating her own circumstances and experiences at the age of fifteen, Mazer is able to remember, and to vividly evoke, what it feels like to be fifteen.

Without: The Author and Her Readers

Norma Fox Mazer has gone from earning her living by writing pseudonymous stories and articles for magazines to being a writer who writes what she chooses—novels and stories—for her appreciative young readers. She has succeeded in producing fiction that is not only entertaining, but thought-provoking and meaningful to her readers.

Norma Fox Mazer loves to write. "I go down to my office," she says, "and I sit down and I feel good. It's wonderful." It gives her a lot of pleasure, but she isn't satisfied with just telling a story, to entertain. More than just a story, she says, "A writer wants more. . . . Writer and reader both press on toward the ending to find out what happens and what it signifies."[2] A book written only to entertain, she says, without something worth saying underlying the story, will have a robotlike quality. It will lack the heart beating at its center that is so necessary for a story to be more than a diversion, that will keep the story living in the reader's mind.[3]

Selecting her favorite of her own books is difficult for Mazer, but she chooses *Saturday, the Twelfth of October*. She loved setting up the matriarchal society with its celebration of the menarche. She is also pleased with *Three Sisters*, saying, "I feel this might

even be one of the best books I've ever done. I really feel happy
with the book."

Reflecting on how reviews can depress her if they are negative,
she comments, "My ideal in writing is to write a book that's
intelligent and well written, but popular, and sometimes those
things are at war with each other. I want the readers, I want the
kids, but I also want the reviewers, I want the adults. Naturally
I want everything," she laughs.

Mazer wants young people to like her books, so she writes the
kind of books she would like to read herself. She finds it really
hard to find a book that she loves. She's "addicted" to the *New
York Times Book Review*. They are always praising books that
she runs out and gets, and then she thinks, "Come on, these people
can write circles around me, but it's boring." She talks about one
writer who is "very polished": "She's kind of like her books. . . .
You sense that there's something there, but there's such a thick
layer between *her* and *her*. She's very polished and her books are
very polished and yet they never warm me."

She loves a writer who can really write well, but what she wants
to read is realistic fiction, like Alison Lurie's *Foreign Affairs*.
What Mazer looks for in contemporary fiction is what she tries
to create in her own books—a view into the lives of others, ex-
pressed by her image of looking into a window, face pressed up
against the glass:

> Gradually the lights will go on in every room, and we will be
> privileged to see what's happening there. How people talk to
> each other, what they do, how they love and hate, and make
> up and cry, and try and fail, and try again.[4]

Mazer's future plans include a book for adults, which she drafted
in the summer of 1985. She has always shown a desire to do
different kinds of writing. "Much as I love writing for young
people," she says, "there's still a limitation on what you can do."
She adds that she would never give up writing for young people.

In addition to wanting to write for adults, she is working on
books for younger girls. She wants them to be lighter than her

young adult books and amusing. "I seem to get very, very serious when I write my books and it bothers me," she comments. "Everybody wants to do the thing that they don't ordinarily do." When she wrote *Downtown,* her intention was to write a "light" book. She would have her two characters, a boy and a girl, meet downtown, and she'd set it in her town. She decided that they were each to have a secret. She began knowing what Cary's secret would be—her parents' past. But she didn't figure out, right away, what Pete's secret would be. Her agent, Elaine Markson, suggested in a discussion, "What if his parents were underground?" and Mazer knew "instantly" that that was right for the book. So, instead of writing something light, she found herself getting into something very serious. She loved writing the book because it presented her with a lot of moral questions that she had to think about. Pete's parents are peace activists, but their actions end in violence. She still feels, though, that she wants to write something lighthearted, so she came up with the idea of doing books for younger children, aged about eleven to thirteen. Of course, she adds, "naturally they'll be about something, they have to be about something."

Mazer is also interested in how her books reach her readers. *Taking Terri Mueller* was an unusual book because it was first published in paperback rather than being issued in hardcover first and in paperback later, as is customary. Jean Feiwel, Mazer's editor, planned to start a line of good original paperbacks. At the time, journals like *School Library Journal* had begun for the first time to review original paperbacks. Mazer was anxious about publishing in paperback first, but liked the theory of the experiment. She thought that paperbacks were important to kids because the prices of hardcover books were too high. She thinks the paperback *Taking Terri Mueller* was overlooked in a number of places where her hardcovers are always noticed, but it won honors like the Edgar Allan Poe Award and the California Young Readers Medal and was later bought by Morrow for a hardcover version for the library market. Some of her books have been published simultaneously in paperback and hardcover. Mazer is happy with this unusual arrangement because her readers can get her books in paperback at the same time that the libraries have them in hard covers.

As mentioned above, Mazer wants her books to be both respected by adult reviewers and liked by teenage readers. *Dear Bill, Remember Me?* is an example of a Mazer book that received both critical and popular success. Critic Pamela D. Pollack called the stories "Quiet and unaffected . . . fiercely felt renderings of misplaced love and search for selfhood."[5] It was named an outstanding book of the year by the *New York Times* and a Best Book for Young Adults by the American Library Association. It also received a Christopher Award, given annually by the Christophers to books representing a high level of human and spiritual values.

Teenagers liked the book, too. In a school Mazer visited, a girl came up to her with a battered, ripped, coverless copy of *Dear Bill.* She asked Mazer to autograph it and when Mazer asked about its condition, the girl told her that fifty-seven kids had read the book. Mazer asked the girl if she would swap it for a new copy. She asked the girl to sign the old paperback, and she wrote, "Mrs. Mazer, we liked this book so well that 57 of us read it."

Mazer receives a lot of fan mail. Sometimes a teacher asks her class to write to their favorite authors, and she gets a lot of those assignment letters, but, she says, every once in a while she gets a great letter. She used to write a response to every letter, a practice she now calls "berserk." She does try to scribble a note on a form letter to everyone who writes, however. One special letter, she recalls, was from a girl who read *Mrs. Fish, Ape, and Me, the Dump Queen* and asked, "Did you get called names when you were growing up?" She was an overweight little girl and came from a small town. Mazer says there was a lot of heart in that letter.

One thing her readers like to do is suggest different endings to her books. They suggest happy endings that tie everything up, but, Mazer says, if she had done things that way, they wouldn't like the books so much. They even suggest that she write sequels, and although she did write about the *Figure of Speech* character Jenny Pennoyer in a second novel, she has no plans to do sequels.

Mazer manages, in her stories and novels, to explore questions crucial to her readers, and to succeed in entertaining them at the same time.

She has a special talent for creating realistic teenage girl characters and is a tireless experimenter with forms and points of view. Her messages (that life is hard but that one has the strength to survive; that independence is necessary and positive; that one can cope with being an outsider; and that living the truth is far preferable to hypocrisy) are meaningful and heartening.

Her interests, her intellectual curiosity, and her talent make her a unique writer in the young adult field.

Notes and References

Chapter 1: Norma Fox Mazer and the Roots of Realism

1. G. Robert Carlsen, *Books and the Teenage Reader: A Guide for Teachers, Librarians and Parents*, 2d rev. ed. (New York: Harper & Row, 1980), 57.
2. Ibid., 58.
3. Kenneth L. Donelson and Alleen Pace Nilsen, *Literature for Today's Young Adults* (Glenview, Ill.: Scott, Foresman, 1980), 185.
4. Sally Holmes Holtze, ed., *Fifth Book of Junior Authors and Illustrators* (New York: H.W. Wilson Co., 1983), 204.
5. Barbara Wersba, review of *Saturday, the Twelfth of October, New York Times Book Review*, 19 October 1975, 12, 14.

Chapter 2: Evolution of an Artist

1. Lou Willett Stanek, "Growing Up Female: The Literary Gaps," *Media and Methods*, September 1976.
2. Donelson and Nilsen, *Literature for Today's Young Adults*, 37.
3. Jill Paton Walsh, review of *A Figure of Speech, New York Times Book Review*, 17 March 1974, 8.
4. Barbara Wersba, review of *Saturday, the Twelfth of October, New York Times Book Review*, 19 October 1975, 12, 14.
5. Ibid.
6. Patty Campbell, review of *Up in Seth's Room, Wilson Library Bulletin*, October 1979, 123, 139.
7. Review of *Up in Seth's Room, Kirkus Reviews*, December 1979, 1380.

Chapter 3: The Craft of the Short Story

1. Robert S. Gold, ed., *Point of Departure: 19 Stories of Youth and Discovery* (New York: Dell, 1967).

2. Charlotte Zolotow, sel., *An Overpraised Season: 10 Stories of Youth* (New York: Harper, 1973).

3. Donald R. Gallo, ed., *Sixteen: Short Stories by Outstanding Young Adult Writers* (New York: Delacorte, 1984), introduction.

4. Edgar Allan Poe, "Review of *Twice-Told Tales* by Nathaniel Hawthorne," in *Great Short Works of Edgar Allan Poe* (New York: Harper & Row, 1970), 522.

5. Deborah Hautzig, *Second Star to the Right,* (New York: Greenwillow, 1981), 37.

6. Edith Wharton, *The Writing of Fiction,* (New York: Scribner's, 1925).

7. Edgar Allan Poe, 521.

Chapter 4: The Message

1. *Taking Terri Mueller* (New York: Avon/Flare, 1981), backmatter.

Chapter 5: Within and Without

1. Dorothy Briley, "Publishing for the Young Adult Market," in *Libraries and Young Adults: Media, Services, and Librarianship,* ed. JoAnn V. Rogers (Littleton, Colo.: Libraries Unlimited, 1979), 18.

2. "Growing Up with Stories," *Top of the News,* Winter 1985, 167.

3. Ibid., 163.

4. Ibid., 167.

5. Pollack, Pamela D., *School Library Journal,* October 1976, 119.

Selected Bibliography

Primary Sources

1. Novels

A, My Name Is Ami. New York: Scholastic, 1986.
Downtown. New York: Avon, 1984.
A Figure of Speech. New York: Delacorte, 1973.
I, Trissy. New York: Delacorte, 1971.
Mrs. Fish, Ape, and Me, The Dump Queen. New York: Dutton, 1980.
Saturday, the Twelfth of October. New York: Delacorte, 1975.
The Solid Gold Kid (with Harry Mazer). New York: Delacorte, 1977.
Someone to Love. New York: Delacorte, 1983.
Supergirl. New York: Warner Books, 1984.
Taking Terri Mueller. New York: Avon, 1981.
Three Sisters. New York: Scholastic, 1986.
Up in Seth's Room. New York: Delacorte, 1979.
When We First Met. New York: Four Winds/Scholastic, 1982.

2. Short Stories—Collections

Dear Bill, Remember Me? and Other Stories. New York: Delacorte, 1976.
Summer Girls, Love Boys and Other Short Stories. New York: Delacorte, 1982.

3. Short Stories—Individual

"I, Hungry Hannah Cassandra Glen. . . ." In *Sixteen: Short Stories by Outstanding Young Adult Writers,* edited by Donald R. Gallo. New York: Delacorte, 1984.
"Tuesday of the Other June." In *Short Takes: A Short Story Collection*

for Young Readers, selected by Elizabeth Segel. New York: Lothrop, Lee & Shepard, 1986.

4. Articles and Speeches

"Censorship and the Writer." *ALKI* (Washington Library Association Journal) 2, no. 2 (July 1986). From a speech delivered to the Washington Library Association in October 1985.

"Comics, Cokes & Censorship." *Top of the News* 32, no. 2 (January 1976). Reprinted in *Library Lit. 7—Best of 1976.* Edited by Bill Katz. Metuchen, N.J.: Scarecrow Press, 1977.

"Growing Up with Stories." Speech at Young Adult Services Division luncheon, American Library Association Conference, 24 June 1984, Dallas, Texas. Reprinted in *Top of the News* 41, no. 2 (Winter 1985).

"I Love It! It's Your Best Book!" *English Journal* 75, no. 2 (February 1986).

Interview by Frank McLaughlin. *Writing!* 7, no. 7 (March 1985).

"Up in Seth's Room: Some Thoughts." *ALAN Review* of the National Council of Teachers of English 8, no. 1 (Fall 1980).

"When You Write for Young Adults." *Writer* 99, no. 2 (February 1986).

Secondary Sources

1. Books and Pamphlets

Carlsen, G. Robert. *Books and the Teenage Reader: A Guide for Teachers, Librarians and Parents.* 2d rev. ed. New York: Harper & Row, 1980.

Donelson, Kenneth L., and Alleen Pace Nilsen. *Literature for Today's Young Adults.* Glenview, Ill.: Scott, Foresman & Co., 1980.

Holtze, Sally Holmes, ed. *Fifth Book of Junior Authors and Illustrators.* New York: H. W. Wilson Co., 1983.

Lukens, Rebecca J. *A Critical Handbook of Children's Literature.* Glenview, Ill.: Scott, Foresman, 1976.

Rudman, Masha Kabakow. *Children's Literature: An Issues Approach.* 2d ed. New York: Longman, 1984.

Stanek, Lou Willett. *A Study Guide to Two Novels by Norma Fox Mazer.* New York: Avon, ca. 1981.

Turnbull, Colin M. *The Forest People.* New York: Simon and Schuster, 1961.

Varlejs, Jana, ed. *Young Adult Literature in the Seventies.* Metuchen, N. J.: Scarecrow Press, 1978.

Weiss, M. Jerry, ed. *From Writers to Students: The Pains and Pleasures of Writing.* Newark, Del. International Reading Association, 1979.

Wharton, Edith. *The Writing of Fiction.* New York: Scribner's, 1925.

2. Articles

Briley, Dorothy. "Publishing for the Young Adult Market." In *Libraries and Young Adults: Media, Services, and Librarianship,* edited by JoAnn V. Rogers. Littleton, Colo.: Libraries Unlimited, 1979.

Pickering, Samuel, Jr. "The Function of Criticism in Children's Literature." *Children's Literature in Education* 13, no. 1, Spring 1982.

Poe, Edgar Allan. "Review of *Twice-Told Tales* by Nathaniel Hawthorne." In *Great Short Works of Edgar Allan Poe.* New York: Harper & Row, 1970.

Pollack, Pamela D. "The Business of Popularity: The Surge Of Teenage Paperbacks." *School Library Journal* 28, no. 3, November 1981.

Stanek, Lou Willett. "Growing Up Female: The Literary Gaps." *Media and Methods,* September 1976.

Index